1977

MACBETH, KING LEAR

AND

CONTEMPORARY HISTORY

MACBETH, KING LEAR
& CONTEMPORARY HISTORY

BEING A STUDY OF THE RELATIONS OF THE PLAY
OF *MACBETH* TO THE PERSONAL HISTORY OF JAMES I,
THE DARNLEY MURDER AND THE ST BARTHOLOMEW
MASSACRE AND ALSO OF *KING LEAR* AS SYMBOLIC
MYTHOLOGY

BY

LILIAN WINSTANLEY, M.A.

1970
OCTAGON BOOKS
New York

First published 1922

Reprinted 1970
by permission of the Cambridge University Press

OCTAGON BOOKS
A DIVISION OF FARRAR, STRAUS & GIROUX, INC.
19 Union Square West
New York, N. Y. 10003

LIBRARY OF CONGRESS CATALOG CARD NUMBER: 74-120680

PREFACE

I WISH, as before, to thank my historical colleagues at Aberystwyth—Mr Sydney Herbert, Dr E. A. Lewis and Professor Stanley Roberts—for the invaluable assistance they have given me in recommending books and sources and in discussing this work during its progress. I wish especially to thank Professor Stanley Roberts for a particularly generous encouragement, of the more value because of his own wide knowledge of Elizabethan history.

I also desire to express my gratitude to Mr Hubert Hall of the Record Office for his very kind assistance during my work there.

To readers who are interested in these studies of Shakespeare so far as they have gone I should like to say that the evidence will be cumulative, each study confirming its predecessors. Thus, in searching for contemporary parallels to *King Lear* I had the good fortune to find a book, Pierre Mathieu's *Deplorable Death of Henry IV*, with its accompanying Panegyric and Poem, which I take to contain a far-reaching explanation of the allegory of *The Tempest*; extracts from this book are given in Chapter XIV of the present work and in Appendix B. I intend to make it the subject for my next study and I should like to say that it will give the strongest corroborative evidence for the treatment of *King Lear* as symbolic mythology.

L. WINSTANLEY.

ABERYSTWYTH, 1922

CONTENTS

MACBETH, KING LEAR
AND CONTEMPORARY HISTORY

INTRODUCTION

IN a previous book entitled *Hamlet and the Scottish Succession* I endeavoured to show that a considerable proportion of the material employed in the play of *Hamlet* was really historical and political in origin. The book met with a larger degree of sympathy than I expected though it inevitably excited controversy.

I propose in the present book to apply the same method to *Macbeth* and *King Lear*, i.e., I propose to consider these two plays in relation to contemporary history.

My main assumption is that, as Shakespeare wrote the plays for a definite audience at a definite point of time, we cannot hope to understand them fully without asking first and foremost what they would mean for that audience. A dramatic poet appeals first and foremost to the mentality of his audience and it is through the mentality of his audience that his plays must consequently be interpreted.

Shakespeare did not write for the men of the twentieth century or for the men of the nineteenth century; he wrote for the men of the sixteenth and the early seventeenth centuries and thus the interpretation that the men of his own day would be likely to place upon his plays is exceedingly important.

I should like to point out that the method is simply the endeavour to bring literary criticism up to date. All criticism depends ultimately upon philosophy and many of our Shakespearean critics, whether they know it or not, are really arguing from a philosophy long since discredited; thus their idea of time is very largely a Cartesian idea of time; according to which it is either non-existent or else so unimportant that it is safe to ignore it. What else do they mean when they speak of Shakespeare as a "universal poet" in the sense of a poet who is equally intelligible to all ages and all periods of time and whose plays would therefore mean the same thing to the men of his own age and to the men of ours. Now to those of us who have studied Bergson this conception of the irrelevance and unimportance of time is quite impossible; we think of time or space-time as of a fundamental reality and of duration as the very stuff of life itself.

The practical application in the sphere of criticism means that it is impossible to dissociate a poet from time and space and consider him simply as he is in the abstract.

Yet this is what much of our Shakespearean criticism really does or attempts to do. Consider, for example, Mr Bradley's book on *Shakespearean Tragedy* which I only choose as an illustration because it represents the high-water-mark of its particular method. Mr Bradley makes a few incidental references to contemporary events but they are singularly few and unimportant; so far as the main substance of the plays is concerned Mr Bradley seems to see no connection whatever between them and the age in which they were written. He might, for all the connection he sees, have met them straying about loose in the age of Pericles or in the period of the Romantic Revival.

The plays were written by an Englishman in the early seventeenth century. What is their relation to space-time, in other words, to England and the seventeenth century?

It is inconceivable that any work can mean exactly the same for all men in all ages.

Let me choose as a parallel case to the method I desire the Higher Criticism of the Bible.

There was a time not so very long ago when the Bible was assumed to be equally true and equally intelligible for all men at all times and, as Ruskin puts the matter, it was so ordained by God in order that we might all understand it. Now this was a very simple and, granting the assumption of a Divine Author, a very logical way of regarding the matter. But let me point out that it was only logical in the case of a Divine Author for no other could be supposed to be so far above space and time. No educated person, however, now thinks of regarding the Bible in that way. The Higher Criticism has taught us to concern ourselves with each book of the Bible individually, to ask ourselves first and foremost at what date each book was written and under what circumstances and what it would mean for the men of that age. Now in the case of the Bible, if anywhere, it might be logical to divorce it from space and time; but, the principle of relativity being accepted even there, what is there to hinder us from applying it in the case of Shakespeare? He cannot be more divine than the Bible?

Now the moment we attempt to apply the principle of relativity to Shakespeare certain very important facts stand out:

1. The Elizabethans and Jacobeans had no newspapers and were not allowed the right of discussing political affairs on the public platform. Consequently they expected the stage to play the part of both newspaper and platform. The stage of Shakespeare's day was continually and closely associated with politics.

2. A rigorous censorship was exercised over the stage. It

was forbidden to represent contemporary monarchs upon the stage even if they were represented in a favourable light. Any individual, whatever his rank, who found himself criticised upon the stage, could apply to the Court of Star Chamber for a veto, and such applications were frequent.

Thus the dramatists had the strongest possible motives (*a*) for representing politics and contemporary history upon the stage, (*b*) for evading the censorship by representing their politics or history in some convenient disguise.

In my previous book I pointed out that the method of Hamlet in dealing with the Gonzago story (i.e. by altering it to adapt it more closely to the circumstances of his father's murder) was precisely the method the dramatists were accused of employing in the case of Essex.

3. Psychology also has its historical development and therefore the psychology of one age cannot exactly resemble the psychology of another. Anyone who wants to know what I mean by these differences can turn either to Mr Gregory Smith's analysis of Ben Jonson's psychology in his *Life of Ben Jonson* or to my own analysis of Spenser's psychology in my editions of the *Faerie Queene* (Bks. I and II). A reader who will refer to these will see that the psychology of both Spenser and Ben Jonson differs extraordinarily from that of the nineteenth century. Now, if we are going to interpret Shakespeare's plays by a psychological method, we ought surely to begin by explaining what his psychology really was. But neither Mr Bradley, nor any other Shakespearean critic known to me, does anything of the kind.

One of my reviewers argued with me that, even if Shakespeare's psychology did differ from ours, it could only differ in unimportant details. But how does he know that, how can he know it, when in the case of Shakespeare's contemporaries the differences are really profound? It has a very considerable practical bearing. Thus in my previous book I developed the thesis that many of the traits in Hamlet were drawn from James I and that others were drawn from Essex. It was objected that this was improbable. But why improbable? It was certainly the method of Spenser's psychology for he nearly always draws his leading characters from more originals than one. Now I do not for a moment argue that Shakespeare's psychology must, of necessity, resemble Spenser's; but, when I find a specific instance in which there is good evidence that it does, I am hardly surprised. Personally I find the resemblances to be important in practically every play and I find the method in *Macbeth* and *King Lear*, at any rate, to be very largely Spenser's, applied far more finely than he applies it, but still his method.

4. The Elizabethans were not only men of the Renaissance but they retained in their mentality a good deal of the Middle Ages and one custom inherited from the Middle Ages was their fondness for symbolism. This is again most obvious in Spenser whose *Faerie Queene* is one mass of symbolism; but it is also very plain in some of Shakespeare's dramatic predecessors, for instance Lyly whose work is a kind of symbolic mythology. Spenser, I may remark, tells us himself that his mythology refers to contemporary events and M. Feuillerat[1] certainly interprets Lyly's mythology in the same way. Everyone is, of course, aware that the mystery and miracle plays, which preceded Shakespeare's stage, were full of symbolism. Now should we not expect on *à priori* grounds to find a certain amount of symbolism in Shakespeare? Would it surprise us if there were a good deal? Let us observe, to begin with, that many of his tales are absurd and fantastic if taken literally; but would be

[1] See A. Feuillerat, *John Lyly.*

admirable if taken symbolically. Mr Maurice Moscovitch, the Jewish actor who rendered the part of Shylock, told me that he found the story of the pound of flesh fundamentally absurd and could not understand why such splendour of character drawing should be associated with such absurdity of action. Now, judging the *Merchant of Venice* as literally interpreted, I can only say that I agree with Mr Moscovitch. But let us observe one fact! The tale of the pound of flesh, though absurd if taken literally, is admirable as a symbol and in that way we employ it every day; when we wish to speak of someone who insists on the whole of a cruelly hard bargain we speak of him as demanding his "pound of flesh." Well! May not Shakespeare have meant it as a symbol from the beginning? I agree with Mr Maurice Moscovitch that, if taken literally, it is absurd; therefore I do not think it can ever have been intended to be taken literally.

Another instance which no one can help taking symbolically is the ass's head applied to Bottom and Titania in love with Bottom so transformed. Here the symbolism is so obvious that no one can miss it and it is impossible to imagine that Shakespeare himself did not see it. The only questions are: Did he mean it to apply to the blindness of love in general? Or to some specific instance of the blindness of love? Or to some specific instance typifying something general? Surely it would be of interest to know the precise meaning of the symbol; but I do not think that, in this case at least, anyone can doubt we have a symbol. Or select as another instance the character of Caliban? Is Caliban a figure in a fairy-tale? Or is he symbolic? If he is symbolic, what does he stand for? Once again let us observe that it is very easy to use him as a symbol. Thus Sir Paul Vinogradoff, wishing to describe the modern Bolshevik rule in Russia, describes it as the "rule of Caliban" and all is said; we know at once what he means.

Shakespeare's plays, as usually interpreted, form a singular mixture of baby-tales combined with some of the profoundest wisdom in the world; as a rule we persist in taking the baby-tales seriously; but I believe that, when we do so, we greatly under-estimate Shakespeare's genius. I cannot, for my part, take literally things like the three caskets story or the pound of flesh story, or Bottom with the ass's head, or Lear's division of his kingdom, or Gloucester and Edgar in the precipice scene, or the trial of the joint-stools by Lear. The three last instances are particularly remarkable because they occur in the greatest of all Shakespeare's tragedies and because they are, as they stand, so palpably absurd.

Hardly anyone denies the absurdity of Lear's division of his kingdom. But critics explain it by saying that Shakespeare found it in his source and did not trouble to alter it. This scarcely seems to me an explanation for the truth is, as I shall show later, that Shakespeare made it much more improbable than it is in the source. In any case the precipice scene and the trial of the joint-stools are equally improbable and Shakespeare did not find *them* in his source; he added them himself.

I believe all three examples to be really symbolism; I shall attempt to explain them in the following pages and I believe that when the true meaning is known it adds greatly to the horror and the tragedy of the drama.

I wish to call attention here, however, to the following facts:

(*a*) That symbolism is very frequent in Shakespeare's contemporaries.

(*b*) That there are a great many scenes and characters in Shakespeare which can be used symbolically and which seem as if they were obviously meant as symbols.

(c) It is more than possible that what seem absurdities in Shakespeare may be simply symbolic.

5. In comparing Shakespeare's plays with contemporary history we must remember that the principle of relativity applies to the history itself and that it would not appear to contemporaries precisely as it appears to us. We must remember that contemporaries estimate individuals much more passionately and very differently, that they admire them more, hate them more, see them in an aspect much more lurid or much more grand or with a pathos we cannot even imagine; we must remember also that historic events, as seen by the eyes of contemporaries, are often curiously different from anything the modern historian imagines. Suppose, for example, that a modern historian were asked to represent the whole massacre of St Bartholomew in a single tableau or picture. Would he represent it as an old man naked in a thunderstorm? I cannot conceive that he would, but the French Huguenots (as I shall show later) certainly represented France suffering from St Bartholomew as an old man, exposed naked to the elements![1] They derived the idea from the terrible tragedy of Coligny. The old man was murdered, his naked body was exposed to all the elements of air and water and fire, and in their French and Latin elegies the French Huguenots symbolise the massacre of St Bartholomew as a great thunderstorm sweeping the land, speak of Coligny as the father of his country exposed by his ungrateful children naked to the tempest and then proceed to identify Coligny with France itself. I shall quote the poems later which show different stages in the development of the idea[2]. The image, which seems so strange to

---

[1] Chap. xiv.

[2] *Memoires de l'estat de France sous Charles IX*, 1576. Anonymous, published by Heinrich Wolf, Meidelbourg; in Chap. xiv.

us, was completely natural to the Huguenots themselves and it would be just as natural to any Englishman who sympathised with them and who knew their point of view.

This, I may remark, is only typical. Symbolic views of history were common in the sixteenth and early seventeenth centuries. I have come across some works, purporting to be history, which were really symbolic interpretations throughout[1].

Let me recapitulate before proceeding further. If we study Shakespeare in close relation to his age the main points to be observed are:

(1) That the Elizabethans and Jacobeans had neither newspapers nor public platform and that the stage was expected to do duty for both, and hence the stage was continuously and closely associated with politics.

(2) That the censorship was very strict, even more strict than the law of libel is to-day, and therefore the dramatists were compelled to adopt some form of disguise.

(3) That the psychology of the sixteenth century must differ, in many respects, from the psychology of the nineteenth, and hence in interpreting Shakespeare we must be prepared for this difference.

(4) That the men of the sixteenth century, alike in poetry and in drama, made a large use of symbolism and that we must therefore be prepared for the use of such symbolism in Shakespeare.

(5) That it was the custom to represent contemporary history in symbolism and that such symbolism, as in the case of the Huguenot representation of St Bartholomew, is often exceedingly powerful and dramatic.

Before proceeding, however, there are two questions which it is very pertinent to ask:

[1] P. Mathieu, *Deplorable Death of Henry IV*, etc., etc.

(*a*) If there exists a real relation between Shakespeare's plays and the history of his time, has not this been suspected before? If so, why have modern critics not worked it out conclusively?

(*b*) Did Shakespeare's contemporaries leave no explanations of his plays? If so, where are they and why have they so long been ignored?

Let us deal first with (*a*).

It is a fact that historical relations have not infrequently been suspected in Shakespeare's plays. Thus Malone frequently calls attention to historical parallels in *Measure for Measure* and elsewhere; it was, as a matter of fact, Malone's notes on *Measure for Measure* (a play I happened to be editing) which first called my own attention to the subject.

Nor was Malone the only person who had previously perceived historical parallels in Shakespeare. Writing about a century ago Plumptre suspected a relation between the Darnley Murder and the murder of Hamlet's father; George Russell French had also found a connection (as I pointed out in my book) between the maxims of Polonius and those of Lord Burleigh. Mr Abbott (whom again I quoted) suggested a similar parallel between Hamlet and Essex as the latter was in his evil days. Other critics, whom I need not quote here, had suggested historical parallels for various plays.

It has even been suspected that Shakespeare's plays were a form of mythology; thus Tieck believed that *A Midsummer-Night's Dream*, *The Merchant of Venice* and *Romeo and Juliet* were all essentially mythology and that they formed a trilogy.

The truth appears to be that the older editors and critics of Shakespeare did, not infrequently, suspect a historical foundation for his plays; but, though they suspected it, they were unable to prove it, and this for two reasons:

(1) They had not sufficient historical material available. Even now the history of the Elizabethan period is most imperfectly studied. There is no detailed and continuous history between that of Froude which concludes with 1588 and Gardiner who commences with 1603[1]. This means that the fifteen years most important for Shakespeare's development, and the years productive of a large number of important plays, are not covered by any detailed history whatever. Moreover there is a paucity even of good biographies; there are very few which are at all comprehensive and many men of eminence in the period have no biographies. The materials my historical colleagues suggested to me as likely to be useful were the publications of the Camden Society, Maitland Club, etc., etc., *The State Papers*, *Venetian State Papers*, Simancas *Archives*, etc., etc. Now, in the early nineteenth century, the Shakespearean student had no Froude, no Gardiner; he had not yet the researches of Mr Spedding, Mr Martin Hume, Mr Abbott, etc., etc. He had no *Cambridge History*. The *Venetian State Papers* had not yet been examined nor the Simancas *Archives*; our own *Domestic and Foreign State Papers* had not been published by the Record Office and many of the publications of our modern antiquarian societies were either inaccessible or at least very difficult of access. I still think that more use might have been made of such historical material as was available; but there was certainly very little.

(2) The earlier students were hampered by the fact that there was no correct time-order for the plays. Let us assume, for the moment, that Shakespeare's plays are partly historical and that they usually refer (as I think they do) to events that for some reason or other are interesting to the

[1] See, however, *Treason and Plot*, by Martin Hume, a study of the last decade of Elizabeth's reign.

audience of that date. These events would, in some cases, be contemporary events as with the Lopez trial and Shylock; in other cases they would be events closely *connected* for some reason or other with contemporary events as the subject of the Darnley murder was closely connected with the accession of James I. It is obvious that, if the historical method of interpretation be possible at all, the correct date must be a clue of the very greatest value and, in many cases, an incorrect date might make the historical interpretation of the play totally impossible. Let me choose as an example *The Tempest*. This play has all the appearance of being some kind of allegory and attempts at such interpretation have frequently been made. But in the folio of 1623, *The Tempest* was placed first amongst Shakespeare's plays and this very naturally imbued the earlier editors and critics with the belief that it was one of the earliest. We now rank it among the latest and date it somewhere about 1610 or 1611.

Let us suppose for the sake of argument that *The Tempest* really is an historical allegory and relates to events occurring somewhere about 1610. In that case the earlier critics of Shakespeare who dated it between 1590 and 1595 could not possibly have interpreted it at all because the events referred to in the play would not then have taken place. I may remark incidentally that I have come across what I take to be a contemporary French interpretation of the allegory of *The Tempest*—a large part of it, at any rate—by the Historiographer-Royal of France and that he does interpret *The Tempest* as referring mainly to Henry IV of France[1].

Assuming for the moment that the Historiographer-Royal is right and that the play does refer to the later years of Henry IV of France, the earlier critics who dated it

[1] P. Mathieu, *Deplorable Death of Henry IV*.

between 1590 and 1595 would be totally unable to interpret it correctly. Their task would be impossible. In fact the time-order of the plays and their approximate dates seem to me of the very first importance in determining their historical bearing. The truth, I repeat, is that the earlier students of Shakespeare often *suspected* a historical connection; but they had the utmost difficulty in *proving* it.

I turn now to question (*b*).

Did Shakespeare's contemporaries leave no explanations of his plays and if so, where are they and why have they so long been ignored?

The answer to this question is again twofold.

(1) Shakespeare's contemporaries did leave explanations of, at any rate, some of his plays; but the censorship made it difficult or impossible to explain them in full so we only find portions of the play given.

(2) Since the plays are historical the explanation is usually made by professed historians or semi-historians who are ignored by our literary students because they do not suspect any connection between Shakespeare and the history of his own time.

The example already given is that of Henry IV's Historiographer-Royal—P. Mathieu. In the book he wrote on the death of his master P. Mathieu certainly seems to me to interpret the allegory of three of Shakespeare's plays: *As You Like It*, the Gloucester part of *King Lear* and *The Tempest*, as referring to Henry IV of France.

In this book I deal with P. Mathieu's interpretation of the Gloucester story in its proper place[1]. If the Historiographer-Royal be right then Orlando in *As You Like It*, Edgar in *King Lear* and Prospero in *The Tempest* all refer, more or less, to Henry IV of France. I had already arrived at that

[1] Chap. xiv.

conclusion before finding P. Mathieu's book. I propose to deal with this problem at some future date. Here I only wish to point out that contemporary explanations of Shakespeare's plays do occasionally exist. No doubt more could be found if a careful search were made[1].

The reasons I have given suffice, I think, to explain why the historical method of interpreting Shakespeare's plays fell into disuse and why the psychological method took its place. Schlegel in Germany, Coleridge and Hazlitt in England, were among the chief expositors of this psychological method. It suited Coleridge exceptionally well. He had, as he himself confesses, hardly any historical interests; he *was* deeply interested in psychology and, as I have just explained, the historical material was not, in any case, available. Coleridge opened a new vein which proved exceedingly fruitful and was followed, as the leading method, for a century.

At the same time there was one serious flaw in the psychological method as usually practised, and it seems to me one of the most startling phenomena in the history of Shakespearean criticism that no one, apparently, suspected it. It is the fact that, as I have already said, psychology also has its historical development. It surely ought to have been fairly obvious that the psychology of the sixteenth century was bound to be different from the psychology of the nineteenth century and it surely ought to have been obvious that these differences might be important and, in any case, called for explanation. Several of my critics thought I was objecting to the psychological method *in toto*. This was very far from being the case. What I did object to was the method of those critics who assumed that the psychology of the sixteenth century was and must be identical with the psychology of the nineteenth and interpreted Shakespeare

[1] See also D'Aubigné's *Les Tragiques* in Chap. xiv.

almost exactly as they would have interpreted Browning. Mr Bradley, for instance, interprets the characters of Hamlet and Ophelia, Lear and Macbeth almost precisely as he might interpret those of Guido Franceschini, Caponsacchi and Pompilia. It never even occurs to him that the method of constructing the characters might be radically different, and that the aim might be different. Spenser, to take a sixteenth century example, uses an individual to represent the genius of a whole country, thus Irena and Belgé are characters in his poem and they signify Ireland and Belgium. He also employs characters who stand both for individuals in history and for the genius of a whole nation : as for instance Orgoglio and Mammon represent both Philip II of Spain and Spain itself.

What is more the method is congenial to the whole mentality of the time, for the French Huguenots employ it in the poems they intersperse in their histories[1]. Coligny is himself and he is also the whole genius of France, naked in a tempest of hate; the Queen Joan of Navarre is herself; but she is also the daughter of France, repudiated for her truthfulness, disinherited for her truthfulness (i.e. as a Protestant), but none the less serving the fatherland to the last breath of her life. These instances from Spenser and from the anonymous Huguenots (I shall quote them more fully later) illustrate the exact process by which contemporary history passed into a sort of symbolic mythology.

Now just suppose for a moment that Shakespeare's psychology *was* that of his contemporaries. Might it not throw a strangely different light on *King Lear*? Is not the drama great enough to be the tragedy of a nation? Might it not be the scream of horror wrung from England's greatest genius as he interpreted the anguish of Civil War in France and

[1] *Memoires de l'estat de France sous Charles IX*, Meidelbourg, 1576.

feared (as did actually happen later) a civil war in his own country?

Even Mr Bradley admits that *King Lear* produces an effect upon him closely resembling that of the *Prometheus Vinctus* of Æschylus and the *Divina Commedia* of Dante. Suppose that it were, like them, a piece of symbolic mythology. Suppose that Shakespeare really did share the mentality of his own contemporaries: the French Huguenots, Lyly and Spenser. Suppose that, as P. Mathieu's book seems to suggest, Shakespeare's plays really were symbolic mythology. Why not? A man really does share the ideas of his own era. A great poet really is a portion of his own age. It is not enough to say of any author that his method is "psychological"; psychology is itself relative to the period in which it occurs.

The psychology of the twentieth century already differs greatly from the psychology of the nineteenth and is giving rise, in France, to a new kind of literature; the authors call themselves "unanimistes" and they try to interpret what they call the "psychology of crowds."

The same argument holds with regard to the past, but in still more accentuated form.

Ben Jonson cannot be judged as if he were George Eliot. Neither is Spenser's method the same as Browning's. In *The Ring and the Book*, for example, Browning aims at drawing actual living human beings and one character stands for one character; Pompilia is an individual Italian girl and she is Pompilia; Guido is a vicious Italian noble, Caponsacchi is an Italian priest, etc., etc.

We should be very much mistaken, however, if we tried to interpret Spenser by such means.

To begin with Spenser's characters are all, in the strict sense, superhuman. Like Aristotle (from whom he learnt so much) he believes that the hero should be greater than life. All his heroes and heroines are really superhuman; they are not portraits, but still less are they fiction; thus the deeds of Artegall are composed of the deeds of Arthur, Lord Grey of Wilton and Lord Leicester; Duessa, again, is a figure of superhuman wickedness and includes both Mary Tudor and Mary, Queen of Scots. Una is a figure of superhuman beauty and includes something of Anne Boleyn and much of Elizabeth.

Now let us ask ourselves the question: Why should Shakespeare's psychology resemble Browning's more than it resembles Spenser's? Let us remember that Spenser's psychology is completely in accord with the genius of his own age. We can actually see the contemporary historians at work turning the history of their own times into a sort of symbolic mythology. Thus the anonymous Huguenots regard Coligny as Coligny and also as the genius of France, robbed of all by his own ungrateful children[1]. P. Mathieu regards Henry IV as Henry IV and also as the genius of France, assuaging all her discords by the music attendant upon his personality.

P. Mathieu also says that the genius of France was so obsessed with folly that he chose his false and illegitimate son (Guise) and cast out his legitimate son (Navarre). In his own blindness and despair the genius of France was about to destroy himself; but the son whom he had disowned, entirely loyal in his misfortune, saved him from destruction. Here again surely we have a piece of symbolic mythology that closely resembles Shakespeare?[2]

Our modern method of interpreting Shakespeare's psychology almost entirely as if it were Browning's results in some startling discrepancies and what I can only call much

[1] Chap. xiv.   [2] Chap. xiv.

"ploughing of the sand." Consider, for example, what Mr
J. M. Robertson says of *Hamlet*:

There is no better illustration of the need for a study of the
genesis of the Shakespeare plays than the endless discussion of
the aesthetic problem of Hamlet. It has continued for two
centuries, latterly with the constant pre-occupation of finding
a formula which shall reduce the play to aesthetic consistency;
and every solution in its turn does but disregard some of the
data which have motived the others.

Mr J. M. Robertson gives in his book *The Problem of
Hamlet* the leading formulae developed by eminent critics
and has no difficulty whatever in showing how extraordinarily different and how mutually contradictory they
are.

But surely, if the attempt to interpret the character of
Hamlet as an "aesthetic consistency" has simply resulted
in two centuries of contradiction (as Mr Robertson asserts),
there must be something wrong in the method of interpretation? That something wrong quite possibly lies in our
ignoring of Shakespeare's own age and the psychology of
Shakespeare's own age.

Now, in my previous book, *Hamlet and the Scottish Succession*, I endeavoured to show that Shakespeare's material
was really historical, that what he was really endeavouring
to do in *Hamlet* was to reflect in dramatic form the events
most *immediately* interesting alike to his audience and to
himself. His hero, so I believed, was never intended to be
a psychological unity in our sense of the term; he was,
probably, like the great figures of Spenser, essentially superhuman and, like them also, his traits were composed from
more than one individual.

I found in him elements drawn both from James I and
from Essex in the latter's tragic later years and I was not
surprised to find Spenser's method, the method of symbolic

mythology, represented in Shakespeare because I knew Spenser's method to be so completely in accord with the mentality of the whole era.

Let us ask ourselves very carefully one question: Do not Shakespeare's greatest figures produce the impression of being larger than life? To me, at least, they certainly do. I feel that Hamlet, Macbeth, Lear and Prospero are all essentially creatures greater than any individual man. And, if Shakespeare were deliberately making figures greater than life-size, he was only in accord with the whole tradition of his time. The religious drama which preceded him dealt with beings who were usually superhuman; some of them were altogether supernatural, most of them were supernaturally inspired; neither the mystery play nor the morality dealt with ordinary human beings, of ordinary stature. If Shakespeare were acquainted with the classical drama (and he must surely have known something of it) he would find gods and demi-gods playing a large part in that drama. If he knew something of Aristotle (and he probably did) he would find in Aristotle's *Poetics* the statement that the tragic hero is greater than life. And then there was, as I have just shown, the practice of Spenser who draws his data from real life but who carefully constructs a world which is greater than real life.

At any rate one thing is certain; that, as Mr Robertson has (so I think) conclusively shown, no psychological interpretation ever has been found for Hamlet which does not contradict some interpretation with data equally good. I doubt if the men of the sixteenth century would have known what we mean by a "psychological unity"; it seems to me they were aiming at something totally different.

A distinguished scholar who agreed with much in my view of Hamlet told me that he found it difficult to believe that the Elizabethans took so much interest in history as my theory, taken as a whole, implied.

My answer to that is twofold.

In the first place we have very strong evidence that the Elizabethans did take a great interest in history. They had a whole series of chroniclers such as Hall, Holinshed, Fabyan and Stowe; they had great antiquaries—Camden for example; some of their chief poets, the authors of *The Mirror for Magistrates*, Spenser, Drayton and Daniel, all employed material which was largely historical; on the stage the chronicle play and the historical play were among the most popular of all forms.

The long series of Shakespeare's historical dramas is itself sufficient to prove that he shared this passion to its fullest possible extent.

Dr Ward[1] has even suggested that the peculiar greatness of Elizabethan drama may be due to its intimate and close connection with British history[2].

The second part of my answer is that we have the strongest evidence that the stage dealt with *contemporary history*.

As I have shown in my previous book, when Essex and Southampton were tried for their lives it was one of the counts of the indictment against them that they had made a political use of the stage, and the company involved was Shakespeare's company and the play involved was one of Shakespeare's plays, i.e. *Richard II*.

The prosecutions of the Star Chamber are alone sufficient to prove that the authorities suspected the Elizabethan stage of being continually and closely associated with politics.

Moreover, since it was illegal to represent any contemporary Christian monarch upon the stage, they were thus

[1] Now Sir Adolphus W. Ward.   [2] *English Dramatic Literature*, p. 218.

compelled to use some form of disguise. Also, as I have tried to show, the dramatic form itself necessitated a good deal of concentration, which concentration involved a re-shaping of the historical material.

In my previous book I have given a number of testimonies to prove the close connection between the stage and Elizabethan and Jacobean contemporary history. I will add a few further testimonies here.

A certain number of dramatists, Marlowe and Chapman among them, brought contemporary history quite openly on the stage. Thus Marlowe wrote *The Massacre of Paris* concerning which Dr Ward says:

> Its chief interest for us may be said to consist in considerations of historical rather than of literary interest. It certainly shows what an English Protestant of Marlowe's fervid type thought—even when the lapse of ten years or so had cooled down the first glow of indignant wrath excited by the event—of the Massacre, its authors and abettors and the principal personages of French and European political life whom it concerned; or, at least, it shows what view on these matters he thought would be acceptable to an English popular audience[1].

There was also a play by Webster entitled *The Guise* which is non-extant[2].

We have, again, Chapman's remarkable series of plays dealing with French history; the two tragedies *Bussy d'Ambois* and *The Revenge of Bussy*, the first appearing in 1607, the scene being laid at the court of Henry III of France who was himself introduced into the action together with the Duke of Anjou and the Duke of Guise. *The Revenge* deals with a continuation of the same subject. Also based on French history are *The Conspiracie* and the *Tragedy of Charles, Duke of Byron, Marshall of France*, which were

[1] *English Dramatic Literature*, p. 355.
[2] Others by Shirley and Dryden. *Ibid.* p. 355.

printed in 1608 and dealt with comparatively recent events, the execution of Byron having taken place in 1602.

It was, of course, a very daring proceeding to represent French history so nakedly on the boards, and the French Ambassador protested against the introduction of his royal master—Henry IV—upon the stage even though in a complimentary light, because of the ordinance forbidding on the stage the representation of "any modern Christian king[1]."

The *Thierry and Theodoret* of Beaumont and Fletcher is another play supposed to contain numerous references to French contemporary history and Dr Ward thinks it possible that the play was a general satire on the regency of Mary de Médici[2]. Dramatists, very naturally, did not limit themselves to France. They were still more desirous to bring on the stage references to contemporary events in their own country and were continually suspected of having done so, sometimes, no doubt, unjustly, but often with disastrous results to themselves. Ben Jonson's *Sejanus* was generally supposed to have been, in part at any rate, a plea for Essex; it certainly appears to me to be a satire on the methods of obtaining evidence employed in the Essex trial.

Ben Jonson and Chapman together made reflections on the Scots in the play of *Eastward Hoe*; several passages gave great offence to Sir James Murray and the authors were arrested. Jonson's own account was that they were in danger of mutilation, of having "their ears cut and noses." Ben Jonson and Chapman were once more imprisoned in 1605 on account of "a play" of name and contents unknown.

Still more audacious was Middleton's *A game of Chess* in which, says Dr Ward:

Middleton ventured to bring on the popular stage more or less veiled representations of the highest personages in the

---

[1] *English Dramatic Literature*, p. 422.   [2] *Ibid.* p. 690.

realm, as well as of a foreign sovereign with whom King James I had long desired to enter into a more intimate understanding[1].

Miss Sheavyn, in her chapter on "Authors and Official Censors[2]," gives some startling examples of the way in which the stage was censored. I could quote much, but I will limit myself to one passage:

The most innocent allusion to current politics was tabooed by a government which knew itself to be menaced by secret enemies on every side....The nature of the political opinions expressed was not the sole ground of condemnation; the offence lay in publishing any opinions upon matters which the Crown considered out of the legitimate range of the subject's criticism....Drama was especially open to criticism, as offering exceptional chances of working upon popular feeling. During the last years of the life of the turbulent favourite Essex, and those immediately following his execution, the authorities were unusually sensitive. Jonson's *Sejanus* and Daniel's *Philotas* both brought trouble upon their authors, being construed as expressions of sympathy with Essex.

Nor was Shakespeare, in this respect, unlike other dramatists; if Lyly, Marlowe, Ben Jonson, Chapman, Middleton and Daniel all desired to allude to political matters, Shakespeare certainly did the same:

"In Henry V," says Dr Ward, "acted at the Globe Theatre in 1599, Shakespeare referred with sympathetic emphasis to Essex....Irish Expedition then in progress....The references to the Essex plot in Henry VIII hardly admit of doubt."

As I have shown before *Henry IV* and *Richard II*[3] had both, *undoubtedly*, political connections. And now let me sum up before proceeding.

The principal points to observe are these:

(1) Shakespeare's earlier editors and critics did frequently

---

[1] *English Dramatic Literature*, p. 497, etc.
[2] *The Literary Profession in the Elizabethan Age*, pp. 524–536.
[3] *Hamlet and the Scottish Succession.*

suspect a historical foundation for portions, at any rate, of his plays.

(2) A historical interpretation was, however, hindered by the fact that, in the early nineteenth century, very little historical material was available. The history of the Elizabethan period is, even now, comparatively little studied.

(3) The earlier critics had what we now know to be a wrong time-order for the plays and this must have greatly hindered the application of what historical material they possessed.

(4) The extreme difficulty of applying a historical method explains why for so long a psychological method of study was preferred as being the only method available.

(5) This psychological method was, however, applied too indiscriminately because no allowance was made for the inevitable differences between the psychology of the sixteenth century and that of the nineteenth.

(6) The psychology of Spenser—Shakespeare's greatest contemporary—as applied in his poem, differs very greatly from that of any nineteenth century author; it is, however, closely in accord with the historical writing of the age; Spenser employs a kind of symbolic mythology and contemporary history easily passes into just such a symbolic mythology.

(7) There is much in Shakespeare which closely resembles such symbolic mythology and it is more than possible, since it is closely in accord with the spirit of his age, that he also employs it.

(8) The Elizabethan and Jacobean stage was closely associated with politics. Many of the dramatists—Lyly, Marlowe, Chapman, Ben Jonson, Middleton, Daniel, etc.—are known to have produced political plays or to have been prosecuted for political reasons.

(9) Shakespeare's own company was twice involved in
political difficulties on account of Shakespeare's own plays
and, when Essex and Southampton were tried for their lives,
one of the indictments against them was that they had employed Shakespeare's company for political purposes.

(10) The Elizabethans were accustomed to a stage which
in the miracle and mystery plays, and in Lyly, dealt with
the symbolic, and Lyly had certainly used this symbolism
to express contemporary politics[1].

Now in my previous book I endeavoured to study the
play of *Hamlet* from the point of view of the Elizabethan
audience and to make out, as exactly as I could, what it
would mean for them. In this book I shall endeavour to
perform the same task for *Macbeth* and *King Lear*.

In both I arrive at the same conclusion that Shakespeare
is employing in these plays a large element of contemporary
history, that in each case it was history which had a close
and relevant connection with immediate events.

I cannot myself see that there is anything improbable in
supposing that Shakespeare wrote about the events which
interested him most.

Moreover, since he was a popular dramatist of very great
appeal, he would probably write about the things which
interested his audience most. Why should he not?

Assuming the ordinary method of interpretation to be
correct it has always seemed to me difficult to understand
why Shakespeare's tragedies should ever have achieved so
profound and dreadful an intensity. What was there in
their subjects to suggest such dreadful and painful emotion?

Hamlet deals with a tale of early Denmark, not con-
ceivably of any great interest to the poet or his audience;
moreover the original (as I have shown before) is an entirely

[1] A. Feuillerat, *John Lyly*.

different story; The Amleth saga might almost be headed "The Triumph of the Iron Will"; Amleth is remarkable mainly for his iron will; against the most formidable odds he succeeds in avenging his father's murder, in making a most successful marriage and in gaining for himself the crown. Now, why should Shakespeare take this story, turn it inside out and then get so passionately interested in the result? I can understand anybody being interested in "The Triumph of the Iron Will" because it really is a fine subject, but it is the exact opposite of Shakespeare's subject which is much rather, as everybody has seen, the tragedy of the weak will.

The case is quite as peculiar or even more peculiar with regard to *King Lear*. It is admitted to be one of the world's greatest tragedies; the intensity of passion which sobs through it is like nothing else conceivable by the human mind; it is a wail of the utmost imaginable human suffering, a scream of the intensest possible human pain. And all about what? About the domestic affairs of a remote king of the bronze age whose tale in the original *was not a tragedy at all*. This again is the crucial point. Shakespeare has turned it inside out just as he did with the Amleth story.

In the original tale Cordelia succeeds in rescuing her father. Lear is restored to his throne and reigns happily till his death. This is the outline of the story as we find it in all Shakespeare's predecessors, Geoffrey of Monmouth, Holinshed, Spenser, etc., and to most of them it seems to possess but a *languid* and *tepid* interest, an antiquarian interest purely, one would judge, from their manner. Note, however, that it was conceived of as quite genuine history and as a really veracious happening.

Now why *should* Shakespeare do anything so extraordinary? He takes the domestic affairs of a remote king of the bronze age which possess an interest mainly antiquarian, he then alters them completely, notwithstanding the fact that they are regarded as veracious history, he turns the story inside out and then writes the most terrific and moving of all modern tragedies on the result. Now why? Is not this improbable? Why should this tale, only of antiquarian interest to Shakespeare's own generation, in the original not a tragedy at all, why should this tale move Shakespeare with an intensity so appalling? I simply cannot conceive that it does. It is something else which moves him and I want to find out what.

Now in my previous book I endeavoured to show that, in the case of *Hamlet*, Shakespeare was really dealing with contemporary history and that the true reason he *wrote* with such terrible intensity was because, in all probability, he *felt* with such intensity.

In this book I shall endeavour to show that the same thing holds true both of *Macbeth* and of *King Lear* and that the real reason why Shakespeare wrote with such a great, with such a terrific, such an appalling intensity was, in all human probability, because he *felt* with such an intensity, because his real subject possessed for him a great, a terrible and even an appalling interest. He terrifies us because he was himself terrified, he tears us with compassion because he was himself torn with compassion, he fills us with horror because he was himself shuddering in every nerve.

I simply cannot conceive of dramas of such intensity written about early Scotland or the remote bronze age. The human mind does not work with that appalling vehemence when it is dealing with the affairs of the bronze age. I cannot *conceive* a man writing such a tragedy as *King Lear* unless he was most *vitally* and most *painfully* interested in the subject and I cannot understand why, on the ordinary interpretation, Shakespeare had any reason to be either.

I propose now to apply the new method to *Macbeth* and to *King Lear* and to see what light a study of historical and political relationships throws upon these plays. I hope to show in the case of *Macbeth*:

(1) That the play has a definite relation to the political situation at the time it was written, ànd the theme was probably suggested by the Gunpowder Plot which was supposed to be aimed (*a*) at the Protestant Ruler of Britain, (*b*) at the Union of the Crowns of England and Scotland[1, 2].

(2) That the actual story of the hero—Macbeth—has a definite bearing on the subject of the Union of the Crowns since Macbeth was the person who tried to avert the Merlin prophecies and, by trying to avert, fulfilled them[3]. James I was greatly interested in prophecy, especially in prophecies concerning his own career, and such a theme would have been most suitable to represent before him. It was also of the greatest possible interest to an English audience because the Union of the Crowns was then the burning subject of practical politics.

(3) That the Gunpowder Plot was compared by James himself to the very similar plot against his father: i.e. the Darnley murder, and hence that both Shakespeare himself and his audience had been recently and painfully reminded of the Darnley murder[4].

(4) That James I dreaded a repetition of his father's fate and that the populace dreaded it for him[4].

(5) That the murder of Duff by Donwald (which gives the central episode in *Macbeth*) is quoted by at least two contemporary historians[5] as the nearest parallel to the

[1] Gardiner.   [2] Chap. I.   [3] Chap. I.
[4] Chap. II.   [5] Belleforest and Adam Blackwood.

Darnley murder to be found in the annals of Scotland. Now the murder of Duff by Donwald is introduced by Shakespeare (wholly out of its place in Holinshed) into the midst of a totally different reign—the reign of Macbeth, and he probably misplaced it in this way because he wished to depict on the stage a close parallel to the Darnley murder[1].

(6) That Shakespeare modifies the account of the murder of Duff by Donwald so as to make it much more closely resemble the Darnley murder, that certain details appear to have been taken from Buchanan's *Detection* and the *Oration* appended and certain others from the actual depositions at the trial[2].

(7) That the character and practices of Macbeth bear very close resemblances to the character and practices of Francis, Earl Bothwell—the half-mad Stuart cousin of James I, who pursued the king's life by means of witchcraft, who tried to obtain prophecies of his death by means of witchcraft, who consorted with outlaws and broken men and who was both condemned and excommunicated for practising with witchcraft[3].

(8) That the Macbeth of Shakespeare far more closely resembles Francis, Earl Bothwell than he resembles the Macbeth of Holinshed[3].

(9) That the details of the witch scenes in *Macbeth* can all be most closely paralleled by details of the actual Scottish witch-trials in several of which James himself took part and the majority of which were supposed to be aimed directly against his life[4].

(10) That James I all his life believed himself specially

---

[1] Chap. II.   [2] Chaps. III and IV.

[3] *Scottish State Papers* and Pitcairn's *Ancient Scottish Criminal Trials*, in Chap. V.

[4] *Scottish State Papers, Proclamations and Criminal Trials*, in Chap. VI.

persecuted by the powers of evil, witches, wizards and nefarious spirits—led and instructed by Satan in person because he—the king—was the destined and prophesied heir to a restored Arthurian Empire and a united Protestant Britain[1].

(11) That the Privy Council of Scotland believed that the Gunpowder Plot itself was planned by the evil spirits of Scotland (directly inspired by Satan) and wrote James a congratulatory letter on his escape from the said Satanic plot[2].

(12) That the Gunpowder Plot was compared by the people of England at large to the massacre of St Bartholomew and that the populace feared a similar massacre of Protestants in England[3].

(13) That the play of *Macbeth* contains a number of details not to be found in Holinshed but closely resembling details of St Bartholomew, especially of the Coligny murder[4].

(14) That much in the study of Macbeth himself resembles the remorse and terror and hallucinations which are said by contemporary French historians[5] to have haunted Charles IX[4].

(15) That the whole play of *Macbeth* has thus a definite and close relation to the personal history of James I (before whom we know it to have been performed) and to those historical events, i.e. the Darnley murder and the massacre of St Bartholomew, which were then powerfully occupying the minds of the king and the audience because of the supposed resemblance of both to the recent Gunpowder Plot.

[1] *Scottish State Papers, Proclamations and Criminal Trials*, in Chap. VI.
[2] Chap. I.   [3] Chap. II.   [4] Chap. VII.
[5] De Thou and D'Aubigné, also *Memoires de l'estat de France sous Charles IX*.

In other words I think that Shakespeare, in writing *Macbeth*, was appealing just precisely to that complex of emotions which happened at the time to be uppermost in the minds of the king and populace.

Gunpowder Plot appears to us to have been an abortive and a not very serious conspiracy. It did not so appear to the men of that age. It terrified the king because his father had been destroyed by a very similar plot and because he was reminded of all the agonising details of his father's murder: it terrified the English people because a dreadful massacre of Protestants (only too well remembered) had actually occurred in France. The plot also was aimed particularly at the Union of the Crowns and therefore threatened the whole future of the British Empire which the king himself, and possibly the people, believed to have been divinely planned and brought about to counteract the influence of Spain and the Pope in earthly affairs. Moreover both the king and his Scottish Privy Council believed that he had all his life been the object of persecution by witchcraft and that this crime of Gunpowder Plot also resulted from the direct intervention of the same evil spirits. *Macbeth* is a drama ideally calculated to appeal to this peculiar complex of emotions. It is also more than probable that Shakespeare felt this complex of emotions himself and was therefore writing of what interested him most.

In the case of *King Lear* I hope to show:

(1) That, as the drama belongs to the same period as *Macbeth* so also does it appeal to the same complex of emotions as *Macbeth*.

(2) That a large portion of *King Lear* is derived from the story of the Darnley murder, especially as narrated by

Buchanan[1], and that another large portion is derived from the story of St Bartholomew, the death of Coligny and the Civil Wars in France as told by contemporary French historians, more particularly the Huguenots [2].

(3) That these two crimes had already been united and told as one story by the Huguenots[3] who considered that both were due to the machinations of the Catholic League and were the crimes of the House of Lorraine. The Darnley murder, a full account of it as a crime of the House of Lorraine, had already been inserted by these historians into the midst of the affairs of France.

(4) That the Darnley murder was generally described as a "parricide" and that the murder of Coligny was described by contemporary historians as "the greatest parricide in history." Both have thus obvious affinities with *King Lear* which is certainly the greatest parricide in literature[4].

(5) That Darnley held the title of king; that, in spite of his subordinate position, he passionately desired the power of a king, and that he was bitterly humiliated because he was not treated as a king[5].

(6) That Buchanan and the author of the *Oration* accuse Mary, Queen of Scots, of hating the king who, all the time, deeply loved her and only desired her society; of repeatedly repulsing him when he rode with a train to follow her; of giving orders to the Earl of Murray's wife to repulse him; of robbing him of all resources and depriving him of his servants; of turning him out "naked" in inclement weather; of forcing him to take refuge in a broken-down and poverty-

---

[1] Chaps. x and xi.

[2] *Memoires de l'estat de France sous Charles IX*; Pierre Mathieu, *Deplorable Death of Henry IV*; D'Aubigné, *Les Tragiques*.

[3] *Memoires*.   [4] Chap. x.

[5] *Scottish State Papers*, in Chap. x.

stricken hovel where he had only beggars for his consorts; of condemning him to wander, cast off and forsaken by all, deprived of necessities, on the wild heaths of Scotland[1].

(7) That the love-story of Edmund and his wooing of the two sisters—Goneril and Regan—is almost exactly like the story of Bothwell in relation to Mary, Queen of Scots, and his own wife—Lady Bothwell, as told by Buchanan and the author of the *Oration*[2].

(8) That both Mary and Bothwell's wife wrote love-letters to him in rivalry, that they were intensely jealous of each other, and that Mary was suspected of having poisoned Bothwell's wife[3].

(9) That Bothwell wished it to be believed that Darnley had perished in a thunderstorm and that his clothes had been stripped from him by lightning[4].

(10) That the Huguenot historians describe Coligny as the "father" of his country, betrayed by his excessive trust in his ungrateful children[5].

(11) That Coligny was termed "father" by the royal family of France who flattered him grossly, professed the greatest possible reverence for him and murdered him. That the Queen Joan of Navarre was termed "Sister" by the same royal family of France; but that she saw through their flatteries and had no trust in them[6].

(12) That Coligny's dead body was exposed to the most frightful outrages: thrown in the Seine, hanged on a gallows, a fire lit beneath, and that the Huguenot historians in their elegies represent this by saying that the father of his country

---

[1] Chap. XI.   [2] Chap. XII.

[3] *English State Papers*, Foreign Series, in Chap. XII.

[4] Melville's *Memoirs*, in Chap. X.

[5] *Memoires de l'estat de France sous Charles IX*, in Chap. XIV.

[6] Chap. XIII.

was exposed by his ungrateful children naked to the elements of fire, air and water[1].

(13) That the Huguenots further identify Coligny with France itself and St Bartholomew with a tempest which is both thunderstorm and hurricane; they identify the outrages heaped on the naked body of Coligny with the sufferings of France exposed naked to the thunderstorm and hurricane of St Bartholomew[1].

(14) That the Huguenots describe (in their poems) Queen Joan of Navarre as the true and loyal daughter of her country, who could not flatter the royal family of France, who was repudiated for her truthfulness (i.e., because she persisted in keeping to the Protestant faith), who was disinherited for her truthfulness (i.e., because of the excommunication depriving her of her kingdom) and who, none the less, served her fatherland to her last breath and was murdered in serving it[2].

(15) That P. Mathieu, the Historiographer-Royal of Henry of Navarre, describes his master as the legitimate and loyal son of France whom France repudiated in favour of the illegitimate and disloyal son (Guise); none the less Henry served his fatherland, through many privations, generously and forgivingly and, when his fatherland in blindness would have cast itself to destruction, he rescued it[3].

The truth appears to me to be that a good many of the historians of Shakespeare's age: Buchanan, the writer of the *Oration*, P. Mathieu, the French Huguenots, de Thou, D'Aubigné, naturally thought in a kind of symbolic mythology. We cannot take quite literally Buchanan's repeated assertion that Darnley was turned "naked out of doors," robbed of his servants, and turned out to take refuge in a

---

[1] *Memoires de l'estat de France sous Charles IX*, in Chap. xiv.
[2] Chaps. xiii and xiv.
[3] *Deplorable Death of Henry IV*, in Chap. xiv.

hovel with beggars or to wander "naked" on the wild heaths
of Scotland. These things are not literally true, but they
express what Buchanan thought the essence of the situation; they are magnificently dramatic and they would, quite
easily and quite naturally, be employed on the stage.

Similarly it is not literally true to say that Joan of Navarre
was repudiated and disinherited by her fatherland for her
truthfulness, that none the less she served it to her last
breath and was murdered while serving it. Yet this is the
way the Huguenots perceived the essence of the subject,
and this again is magnificent drama.

Again it is not literally true to say that Coligny was the
father of his country, that he perished through implicit trust
in his ungrateful children and through his blind confidence
in their flatteries, that they exposed his naked body to a
storm which was both a thunderstorm and a hurricane. Yet
this was the way the Huguenots envisaged the central
situation of St Bartholomew and it is magnificently dramatic.

Let us also notice the way in which contemporaries tend
to concentrate on one or two figures, in dramatic fashion,
and ignore the rest.

Read the actual depositions of the repeated trials for the
Darnley murder and you will see what a large number of
people were concerned, but Buchanan and the *Oration* concentrate all their attention upon two—Mary and Bothwell—
their lonely colloquy before the murder and the knocking
on the door which roused Bothwell from his bed.

So, if we read an account of St Bartholomew in a modern
historian, we find it to be a maze crowded with hundreds of
characters; but let us read the Huguenot elegies and two
figures stand out like colossal statues against a terrific sky;
one is Coligny, the heroic father of his country, flattered by

his unscrupulous children, trusting them implicitly, rejecting the advice of his most faithful friends and betrayed to a doom at which the world shuddered: a glorious creature ruined by his own excess of trust. The other is the figure of Joan of Navarre, repudiated for her truthfulness, disinherited for her truthfulness yet utterly faithful and loyal. And these two figures are bound together by a bond of unswerving loyalty on the woman's part and the deepest personal affection in both. The truthfulness of Joan of Navarre is always contrasted with the false flattery of Catherine de Médici and Marguerite.

And just in the same way Mathieu sees the younger generation, as it were, embodied in Henry of Navarre, sees him as repudiated and as a fugitive most unjustly set aside, sees him also as "naked" and yet unflinchingly loyal in spite of outrage and poverty and, in the end, saving both himself and his fatherland.

I cannot but say that I think such subjects as these fitting subjects for Shakespeare's supreme art. I can find nothing great enough to be the subjects of dramas like *Hamlet* and *Macbeth* and *King Lear*, except the fate of nations and the fate of the world, and that is what I think they essentially are and I maintain that, interpreting them by the mentality of their own age, we certainly find them such.

In the ordinary interpretation I find Lear's division of his kingdom to be a mere baby-tale, quite unworthy to be the starting-point of the most terrific of tragic dramas; but if it typifies the divisions of France in the Civil Wars and the fatal blindness and rashness which led to those divisions, then I think it quite worthy of the supreme drama which follows.

The reader, however, can study the evidence and judge for himself; to me it appears conclusive.

CHAPTER I

THE SUBJECT OF *MACBETH* AND THE
UNION OF THE CROWNS

THE general consensus of opinion is that *Macbeth* was written somewhere about the year 1606. Mr Boas states the case as follows[1]:

The play first appeared in the folios of 1623. It must, however, be at least earlier than April 20th, 1610, for on that day Dr Forman saw it performed at the Globe and recorded the main outlines in his Diary. On the other hand it must be later than the accession of James I in March, 1603, for a number of passages were evidently intended as compliments to the sovereign who had shewn special favour to the Globe Company. Among them are Macbeth's vision of kings, including some that "two-fold balls and treble sceptres carry," and the incident of touching for the king's evil, a power which James claimed as hereditary in the Stuart house.

There is, further, as Dr Herford and others have shown, a definite reference to the trial of the Gunpowder Plot conspirators in the Porter scene.

"The Porter," says Dr Herford, "utters allusive jests on topics of 1606; the phenomenally abundant harvest and the Jesuit Garnet's defence of equivocation at his trial in the spring[2]."

The usually accepted date is, then, some time in 1606, and other indications both of metre and style, agree very well with this estimate.

The date of the play is thus sufficiently well known and the play itself has a certain obvious connection with James I.

[1] *Shakespeare and his Predecessors.*
[2] *Macbeth*: Eversley Edition.

Sir Sidney Lee puts it[1]:

The story was drawn from Holinshed's *Chronicle of Scottish History*, with occasional reference, perhaps, to earlier Scottish sources. But the Chronicler's bald record supplied Shakespeare with the merest scaffolding. Duncan appears in the *Chronicle* as an incapable ruler, whose removal commends itself to his subjects, while Macbeth, in spite of the crime to which he owes his throne, proves a satisfactory sovereign through the greater part of his seventeen years reign.

Only towards the close does his tyranny provoke the popular rebellion which proves fatal to him.

Holinshed's notice of Duncan's murder by Macbeth is bare of detail. Shakespeare in his treatment of that episode adapted Holinshed's more precise account of another murder— that of King Duff, an earlier Scottish king, who was slain by the chief Donwald, while he was on a visit to the chief's castle. The vaguest hint was offered by the chronicler of Lady Macbeth's influence over her husband...every scene which has supreme dramatic value is the poet's own invention....Shakespeare was under no debt to any predecessor for the dagger scene, for the thrilling colloquy of husband and wife concerning Duncan's murder, for Banquo's apparition at the feast, or for Lady Macbeth's walking in her sleep.

The play gives a plainer inclination than any other of Shakespeare's works of the dramatist's desire to conciliate the Scottish king's idiosyncrasies. The supernatural machinery of the three witches which Holinshed suggested accorded with the king's known faith in demonology. The dramatist was lavish in sympathy with Banquo, James' reputed ancestor and founder of the Stuart dynasty; while Macbeth's vision of kings who "two-fold balls and treble sceptres carry" (IV. i. 121) loyally referred to the union of Scotland with England and Ireland under James' sway. The two "balls" or globes were the royal insignia which King James bore in right of his double kingship of England and Scotland, and the three sceptres were those of his three kingdoms of England, Scotland and Ireland.

No monarch before James I held these emblems conjointly.

---

[1] *Life of William Shakespeare.*

Now, before passing on, there are several things to notice here:

(1) It is generally accepted (Mr Boas and Sir Sidney Lee are sufficient examples) that *Macbeth* has a direct connection with James I and introduces direct compliments to him.

(2) That these compliments are closely connected with the Union of the Crowns and bear directly upon it.

(3) That though the main outline of the story is taken from Holinshed that chronicler supplies the baldest scaffolding.

(4) That Shakespeare has inserted in the midst of the story an incident (the murder of Duff) taken from an entirely different reign.

(5) That the character of Macbeth differs markedly from Holinshed's Macbeth and that the scenes which are most important in Shakespeare have not even a suggestion in Holinshed.

These details are important because I hope to show:

(*a*) The reason for every change Shakespeare makes in his source: the insertion of the murder of Duff by Donwald, the change of Macbeth's motive from revenge to ambition, the increased importance of the part played by Lady Macbeth, etc., etc.

(*b*) The true sources of the material not suggested by Holinshed: the colloquy between husband and wife, the knocking at the door, the dagger-scene, the witch-scenes, the Banquo murder scene, etc., etc.

Shakespeare, as I have shown before[1], had an important reason for choosing the subject of Macbeth as such. According to the Merlin prophecies, as interpreted by the Tudor bards, the Arthurian Empire was to be restored and

---

[1] *Hamlet and the Scottish Succession*, Introduction.

the unity of Britain to be achieved when the true British line succeeded to the English throne. Both the Tudors and the Stuarts claimed descent from the ancient British line. The Tudors, as their genealogy by Camden shows, claimed descent from Prince Llewelyn and, through him, from Brutus the Trojan. The Stuarts were similarly derived through Fleance the son of Banquo.

Now, Macbeth knew, for the witches had told him, that the line of Banquo was destined to succeed to the crown; hence his attempt to destroy Banquo and his offspring; but Banquo escaped and fled to Wales to Griffith ap Llewelyn: "To him and Nesta, the Prince's daughter," says Selden, "was issue one Walter....He was made Lord High Stewart of Scotland; out of whose loins Robert II was derived[1]."

Macbeth was really the person who brought about the fulfilment of the Merlin prophecies, and, exactly as happened in the Greek tale of *Œdipus*, he caused the fulfilment of the prophecies by the very means he took to avoid them; it was just precisely his murder of Banquo and his attempted murder of Fleance which caused the flight of Fleance to Wales and his union there with the princess of the ancient British line brought the blood of that British line into the veins of the Stuarts and so to the throne of Scotland.

James I took a keen interest in prophecy, especially such as related to himself, and prided himself greatly on being the destined restorer of the ancient Arthurian Empire. It would thus have been hardly possible for Shakespeare to choose a subject more appropriate to be represented before him and which was calculated to please him better. Moreover, a Jacobean audience would readily understand it because it was so frequent a theme[2].

[1] Notes to Drayton's *Polyolbion*.
[2] See also Drayton's *Polyolbion*, Songs V and X.

Further, we observe the great stress laid on prophecy throughout the play; we see the enormous importance attached to the question of the succession in Macbeth's mind and finally we have the allusion to the unity of the British Isles, the kings who, "twofold balls and treble sceptres carry," and whose line stretches out to the "crack of doom."

Macbeth's anxiety about the succession is somewhat curious as it appears in the play, for we are not shown his children and they do not appear upon the stage.

Now let us put these facts together. Let us observe that the date of *Macbeth* appears to be soon or immediately after Gunpowder Plot, November, 1605, and that the most definite time-reference in the play (i.e. that to Father Garnet's trial) is concerned with that plot. Let us also recollect that the play appears to have a definite bearing on the unity of the British Isles and the restored Arthurian Empire.

James himself believed, and a good many of his subjects believed, that the Gunpowder Plot was aimed against him especially because he had succeeded in uniting the British Isles. He had in this way made Britain the great protagonist of the Protestant faith and incurred the enmity of the Catholic powers. I will give several extracts which bear upon this subject.

The first is a report of the Spanish Council of State to Philip III, February 1st, 1603[1].

Shakespeare cannot have known the deliberations of the Spanish Council of State; but he knew, for all intelligent Englishmen did know, the situation at least as well as the Spaniards and he knew, for all intelligent Englishmen did know, exactly what their conclusions were likely to be.

The extract deals with the question of the succession to the English throne:

[1] Simancas *Archives*.

the introduction of the Infanta and the Archduke involved so many manifestly grave difficulties that it would be better to promote the cause of one of the native claimants, who was a Catholic and might be pitted against the King of Scotland....

The Marquis de Posa added that, if we could not manage to place a Catholic monarch on the English throne it would be better to have any heretic there rather than the King of Scotland who is so pertinacious and badly intentioned in his heresy, because of the power which the united kingdoms would possess if held by so evil a person...the worst solution for us may be regarded as the succession of the King of Scotland. He is not only personally to be mistrusted but the union of the two kingdoms and above all the increment of England in her present position, and with the naval forces she possesses, would be a standing danger to your Majesty in a vital point, namely, the navigation to both Indies. To this must be added the hatred which has always existed between the crowns of Spain and Scotland....

The King of Scotland, moreover, has been badly reared among heretics, and has exhibited in all his actions a false and shifty inclination.

Such a passage is enough to show how intensely the union of the Crowns was dreaded by Spain, and precisely for that reason, i.e. as a weapon against Spain, it was so intensely desired by a large number of Englishmen.

James himself loved tradition and hoary antiquity, and he was particularly anxious to be known as the restorer of the Arthurian Empire. Thus in the *Venetian State Papers*, April 17th, 1603, we find a despatch regarding the new Monarch:

He will stay a few days in Berwick in order to arrange the form of the union of these two crowns. It is said that he is disposed to abandon the titles of England and Scotland, and to call himself King of Great Britain, and like that famous and ancient King Arthur to embrace under one name the whole circuit of one thousand seven hundred miles which includes the United Kingdom now possessed by His Majesty in that island.

When James' poets wished to compliment him they could not compliment him more than on his occupation of Arthur's chair, as in Ben Jonson's *Masque of Queens*: "A night of homage to the British Court and ceremony due to Arthur's chair...the only great true majesty restored in this seat." This plan was not received with equanimity by James' subjects. Neither of his Parliaments approved of carrying the Union as far as the king desired, nor did they wish to merge the names of the separate peoples in that of Great Britain. A good deal of ill-feeling was caused and there was much discontent. On June 4th, 1603, Scaramelli writes:

The ill-will between the English and Scottish goes on rising rapidly. It serves nothing that the king declares his resolve to extinguish both names, and that both people shall pass under the common name of Britons[1].

It was quite commonly believed, not only that the Gunpowder Plot was due to a Catholic conspiracy, but also that it was supported by a number of discontented subjects who disliked the Union and were willing to destroy the king as the chief author and agent of its accomplishment.

Thus in the *Domestic Papers*[2] for November 6th[3], we find an account of how James proposed an interrogatory of one of the accused: "Suggests whether he be not the author of a 'cruel pasquil' against himself for assuming the 'name of Britain' (i.e. King of Great Britain) in which his destruction was prophesied."

Selden also recounts that the Gunpowder Plot was quite generally supposed to be aimed against the Union. Thus in the *Metamorphosis Anglorum* he states:

Elisabetha, Angliae Regina, innupta moritur, Successorem dixit, habuitque Jacobam VI ejus nominis Scotorum Regem,

[1] *Venetian State Papers.*
[2] *English State Papers*: Domestic Series.
[3] 1605.

Magnae autem Britanniae I. consanguinem proximum. Sic
Scotia et Anglia sub uno eodemque Principe conjunctae sunt,
Regnaque Magnae Britanniae novo nomine appellatur. Majori-
bus hostium insidiis expositum et pene oppressum Magnae
Britanniae Regnum fuit, pulvere pyrio in effossam sub Parla-
menti aula humum illato, quo Rex, et soboles Regia, et
procerum optimi quique ac maxime, è medio tollerentur: sed
eae insidiae mox per conscios detectae sunt.

As we have seen, James had further the idea that the
powers of evil were leagued against him to prevent in the
first place his accession to the English Crown and, in the
second place, to destroy him when he succeeded. He was
the champion of Protestantism, he was also the man destined
to unite the British Isles and he quite genuinely believed
in a league against him directly fomented by Satan himself.

Nor must James be accused, in holding this belief, of any
special degree of superstition, or of any special degree of
self-conceit or self-importance, for it was an opinion fully
shared by the principal judges of the Scottish bench and
by the members of James' Privy Council.

I shall return to this question in a subsequent chapter,
but a reference to Pitcairn's *Ancient Scottish Criminal Trials*
as well as numerous proclamations and State Papers make
it abundantly evident that, in the reign of James, there
were repeated trials for witchcraft and sorcery. These evil
practices were supposed to be largely in the hands of
Catholics and to be aimed against James in his capacity as
Protestant heir to England. There was a regular witch's
synod held at Caithness, visited by Satan himself, who instructed his deluded followers how to destroy the king.
Moreover, the men who were James' chief enemies and
whom he certainly believed to be plotting against his life,
i.e. Francis, Earl Bothwell and the Earl of Gowry, were both
accused of sharing in these practices.

James regarded himself and his line as capital objects of dispute between the forces of evil and of good. On the one hand sorcerers, witches and traitors (directly instructed by Satan) were in league to destroy him and his heirs; on the other hand his victory and the victory of his line, and the Union of the British Isles by their means, had been prophesied for centuries before his birth and divine powers were pledged to ensure it.

As I have said the opinion was quite commonly shared by his Scottish subjects, even those in the most eminent positions.

Let us only consider the congratulatory letter which the Privy Council of Scotland sent to James on his escape from Gunpowder Plot and which was dated from Edinburgh, November, 1605. One passage runs:

Since the glad tidings came to us of your Majesty's happy delivery from the abominable conspiracy so inhumanly contrived by the devil and his supporters against your royal person, the Queen and your Majesty's children.

On November 26th, 1605, there was a Proclamation to the Fencibles of Scotland to be in readiness to defend the king which contains the following reference:

this detestable plot which without the concourse of all the devils and malignant spirits within the precinct of this universe, their supporters and deputies upon the face of the earth, could never have been excogitated.

On the subject of the Union, both Masson and Gardiner are interesting and, for our purpose, pertinent. Masson says[1]:

Nothing is more creditable to King James than the strength of his passion for such a union of the two kingdoms and peoples as might fitly follow the union of the two crowns. The intensity

[1] Preface to the *Register of the Privy Council of Scotland.*

of his conception of the desirable union is not more remarkable than its thorough-going generality. For centuries the main island of Britain had been divided politically into an England and a Scotland. There had been fierce war between the two nations and there was still an inheritance of international animosity but, now that the crowns of both nations had been happily united in his own sacred person...was not that a signal that the division and the animosity were henceforward to cease?

What had hitherto been the "Borders" or "Marches" between the two kingdoms were they not now simply the "Middle Shires" of one and the same dominion and ought they not to be re-christened by that name?

Nay, why should the distinctive names of England and Scotland be perpetuated more than reference to the past might make inevitable?

Why should they not be known henceforth as North Britain and South Britain, integral parts of the same Great Britain?...

His right to abolish the name of the "Borders" and substitute that of the "Middle Shires" had been assumed almost since the day of his departure from Scotland. That was a trifle, however, in comparison with his attempt by his own royal authority to abolish the names England and Scotland in all general documents, and to enforce the adoption of the name of Great Britain.

The proclamation alluded to by Masson is that of November 1st, 1604:

Proclamation anent his Majesty's new style and title of King of Great Britain.

James R. Whereas it hath pleased gracious Providence of the Most High in this thrice happy fulness of time, to join and unite in our royal person the two most ancient and famous kingdoms of Scotland and England in unity of allegiance, we think it every way repugnant...

that it which by God and nature's frame was made one (and now to the great joy of so many hearts, united in our person in one invincible monarchy, is one) should any longer retain the memory of the distracted dominions...and seeing nothing is able to procure our better service at home and greater terror to any enemies abroad...we have resolved...that as our im-

perial monarchy of these two great kingdoms doth comprehend, the whole Island...so it shall keep in all ensuing the united denomination of the invincible monarchy of Great Britain... therefore we assume unto ourselves the style and title of King of Great Britain, France and Ireland as our just and lawful style...
discharging and discontinuing the several names of Scotland and England.

Gardiner[1] quotes a passage in the indictment of Guy Fawkes to the effect that

the conspirators should have surprised the person of our Lady Elizabeth and presently have proclaimed her queen, to which purpose a proclamation was drawn, as well as to avow and justify the action, as to have protested against the Union and in no sort to have meddled with religion therein and to have protested against all strangers, that is to say against all Scots. We can readily understand that Privy Councillors, knowing as they did the line taken by the King in the matter of the union would be unwilling to spread information of there being in England a Protestant party opposed to the union, not only of sufficient importance to be worth gaining, but so exasperated that even these gunpowder plotters could think it possible to win them to their side.

Another important point to notice in this connection is that James laid the very greatest stress on the theory of the Divine Right of Kings, in which he earnestly believed, and the best minds of the time were inclined to agree with him because, as both Gardiner and Figgis point out, the claim of the Divine Right of Kings was a very important weapon in the struggle for national rights against the Papacy.

"Before the Reformation," says Gardiner, "the clergy owed a great part of their power to the organisation which centred in Rome, and the only way to weaken that organisation was to strengthen the national organisation which centred in the

[1] *What Gunpowder Plot was.*

crown. Hence these notions of the Divine Right of Kings and of cujus regio ejus religio which, however theoretically indefensible, marked a stage of progress in the world's career...if the religious teaching of the Reformed Church fell, a whole system of earthly government would fall with it."

Mr Figgis[1] has several passages to the same effect. Thus he says:

England was free from papal interference if only she could maintain her position. The battle was not won yet and in this fact lies the justification of mens passionate faith in the Divine Right of Kings. We are too apt to think that from the time of Henry VIII or at least of Elizabeth, the success of the English Reformation was assured. The persistent efforts of foreign powers to convert England, the dreams of so able a man as Gondomar...are alone sufficient proof to the contrary. If all danger of England's submitting to the Papal yoke were over, certainly the fact was unknown at the time either to English statesmen or to Papal diplomatists. England in the time of Henry VIII asserted her claims to independence. A century of statesmanship and conflict were required before they were finally made good. Thus a theory was needful which should express the national aspirations....The English state must assert a claim to Divine appointment.

Figgis says again:

There were many reasons why James I should hold the doctrine of the Divine Right of Kings in its strictest form. His claim to the throne of England rested upon descent alone; barred by two acts of Parliament, it could only be successfully maintained by means of the legitimist principle. Further, it was disputed by the Roman controversialists, who had not sufficient hope of converting James to make them love his title. Doleman's attack upon the hereditary principle is written from the Papalist standpoint.

And again,

In his (i.e. James') True Doctrine of Free Monarchies which saw the light five years before the death of Elizabeth is to be

[1] *Divine Right of Kings.*

found the doctrine of Divine Right complete in every detail. On his accession Parliament passed a statute which purported not to give James a title but merely to declare his inherent right.

In this connection we may refer to the scene in *Macbeth* which introduces the gift of Edward the Confessor in touching for the "king's evil."

The majority of commentators are agreed that this passage, which has no particular relevance where it appears in the play, has been introduced as a compliment to James; but it seems to me to have a really important political bearing, far more than that of a mere personal compliment.

Throughout *Macbeth* Shakespeare's eyes are fixed on the Union of the Crowns; James himself claimed the "peculiar grace" of curing the "king's evil" by touch, and his power in this respect would be taken as a proof of his lineal descent from the kings of England, of the Divine Right of those kings themselves and, further, of James' own Divine Right to the realm.

Obviously the theory of a Divine Right inherent in James would be very much strengthened if it could be proved that secular prophecy had also foretold his advent to the throne. I have already quoted one passage with regard to the Merlin prophecies, but there were many other such prophecies which James appears to have approved.

Thus in the year 1603 there was published a book entitled *Scottish Prophecies*, printed by Robert Waldegrave, printer to the King's most excellent Majesty.

It is described as "the whole prophecy of Scotland, England and some part of France and Denmark, prophesied by marvellous Merlin, Bede, Thomas the Rymer...all according in one."

The most germane for our purpose is the prophecy given under the name of "Sibylla Regina":

...she maketh mention of two noble princes and emperors the which is called Leones, these two shall subdue and overcome all earthly princes to their diadem and crown, and also be glorified and crowned in the heaven among saints. The first of these two is Magnus Constantinus. The second is the ninth king of the name of Steward of Scotland, the which is our most noble king.

There is also a confirmatory prophecy by Thomas the Rymer:

Where dwells thou or in what country, or who shall rule the Isle of Britain From the North to the South Sea? a French wife shall bear the son. Shall rule all Britain to the sea, that of the Bruce's blood shall come, as near to the ninth degree.

We are now in a position to see what the subject of *Macbeth* really meant and with what intensity it must have appealed to the immediate interests and emotions of Shakespeare's audience, and do not let us forget that the king himself is probably appealed to most immediately and directly.

The king is a Scottish monarch and the scene of the play is laid in Scotland. The king prides himself on being the person destined to restore the ancient Arthurian Empire and to unite Britain from the north to the south sea; he believes that his advent has been prophesied from earliest times by Merlin, by Sibylla, by Thomas the Rymer; he believes that God has marked him personally by investing him with the grace of curing the "king's evil" by his touch; he believes that he is destined to preside over a great invincible Protestant power and that, because of this destiny, the forces of evil by means of witches and evil spirits have leagued themselves against him. A terrible plot has recently been discovered aimed partly at the true religion, but mainly at the unity of Britain, and which was intended to destroy the prophesied king and extirpate his prophesied line. Nor are these beliefs peculiar to the king. They are passionately accepted by his subjects. His subjects are, most of them, intensely eager for the Union of the Crowns for they want to strengthen England by this Union in her hereditary struggle against Spain. His subjects are passionately eager to believe in his Divine Right because to claim it for their king is the simplest way of asserting their own right to national development as against the claims of the papacy; therefore his subjects eagerly accept the idea that his advent has been prophesied from the earliest times and that God has given him the divine grace of curing the "king's evil." His subjects also believe that he has all his life been persecuted by the powers of evil who are leagued against him to prevent the growth of the great Protestant Empire; the Privy Council of Scotland are so sure of it that they refer to it as a matter of course in their proclamations and their letters.

And now let us just reflect how ideally suited the subject of *Macbeth* is to appeal to all this complex of emotions.

Its central figure is the man who tried to avert the Merlin prophecies by destroying Banquo and his line and so preventing the restoration of the Arthurian Empire, and who, like the parents of *Œdipus*, only succeeded in fulfilling the prophecy. Throughout the play prophecy is dwelt on as a main motive, and we see the culmination of this prophecy in the succession of the British kings and the permanence of the British Empire, for the kings carry "twofold balls and treble sceptres" and their lines stretch out to the "crack of doom." The witches and evil spirits of the play attempt to destroy Banquo and the line of Banquo—the Stuart kings—just as, in James' own life, they had attempted to destroy him and his heirs. They are foiled as they had been foiled in the life-time of James, and these very powers of evil themselves

4—2

are forced, by a supreme compliment, to give testimony to the permanence of his empire and his line.

Nor must we, in any sense, look upon the play merely as a piece of royal compliment or literary artifice. The subject chosen by Shakespeare profoundly interested the whole nation. The idea of the unity of the British Isles was one that appealed to the best minds of the time; it interested Bacon for instance, no less than James I. Nationalism was the advanced principle of the age, as contrasted with the reactionary doctrine of Papalism, to fight passionately for the nationalist principle meant to fight for freedom of thought against papal supremacy, it meant the possibility of political freedom and political development. British unity meant the achievement of a great Protestant Empire which would ensure freedom of thought and liberty and on which, therefore, there turned the whole freedom of the world.

The true subject of *Macbeth* seems to me to be the furious attempt of the powers of evil to prevent the foundation (or as that age would have put it, the restoration) of the British Empire, to destroy liberty of thought and the freedom of the world.

I think it a great subject and I think we very much underestimate the genius of Shakespeare when we fail to comprehend how vast his subjects really are.

CHAPTER II

THE GUNPOWDER PLOT, THE DARNLEY MURDER AND THE MASSACRE OF ST BARTHOLOMEW

WE, in these modern days, hardly regard the Gunpowder Plot seriously; it was an abortive conspiracy and it was so fantastic in all its details that we can hardly believe there was ever serious danger to be apprehended. But Shakespeare and the men of his time cannot be understood unless we remember that they saw historical events in a quite different perspective from our own and felt them with a quite different intensity.

They certainly took the Gunpowder Plot as seriously as it was possible to take anything. James was, quite inevitably, reminded of the murder of his father; he regarded the Plot as an attempt to make him share a similar fate; it recalled to his mind the ghastly details of his father's murder and filled him with apprehensions of a similar fate.

The English nation, as a whole, were full of horror and consternation; they regarded the Plot as a Catholic conspiracy to destroy the leaders of a Protestant nation and they compared it, very naturally, to St Bartholomew. It was a St Bartholomew which had been foiled, yet it might be the precursor of a new and successful scheme. The likeness to St Bartholomew was increased by the fact that the French ambassador was implicated or was supposed to be implicated; there was no certain evidence of his guilt, but he fled and his flight was justly regarded as an extremely suspicious circumstance. Moreover, he does not seem to have been trusted even in his own country, for Henry IV regarded his conduct as suspicious and declined to receive him.

In this connection we may quote the *Venetian State Papers*; as they were uncensored despatches, they are in some ways a more valuable and veracious picture of the mind of the time than even the *English State Papers* themselves, and they reflect most admirably the emotions of the moment. Shakespeare, we must remember, lived through the moment itself and shared the emotions.

Thus Nicolo Molin writes to Venice:

> About two months ago Lord Salisbury received anonymous letters from France, warning him to be on his guard, for a great conspiracy was being hatched by priests and Jesuits; but as similar information had been sent a year ago by the English lieger in France, no great attention was paid to these letters and they were attributed to the empty-headed vanity of persons who wished to seem more conversant with affairs than became them.

Molin tells the story of the famous letter and says:

> Lord Mounteagle read the letter and, in great astonishment took it to the Earl of Salisbury, who at once carried it to the King.
> ...Meantime, the King read the letter and in terrified amaze he said "I remember that my father died by gunpowder. I see the letter says the blow is to be struck on a sudden. Search the basements of the meeting place."

Thus we see that from the very beginning (Molin writes on November 16th, 1605) it was the common belief that the king had himself detected the plot because of its remarkable similarity in certain details to the plot which culminated in his father's murder.

Molin writes on the subsequent day (November 17th):

> It was a Catholic plot and the king said had it been successful it would have been the most stupendous and amazing event ever heard of....Had it succeeded upwards of thirty thousand persons and those the most prominent would have been slain....

There is also a grave suspicion that the Pope may be the source of the Plot, for, as it is a question of religion, it seems impossible he should not have assented even if he took no active part in it.

...Finally they have a deep suspicion of France whose Ambassador left eight days ago without awaiting his successor. When they learned that on account of the weather, he had not been able to cross the Channel the same night the plot was discovered, they sent orders to Dover that he was not to cross until further instructions.

Molin writes again on November 21st:

The King is in terror; he does not appear nor does he take his meals in public as usual. He lives in the innermost rooms with only Scotchmen about him....Catholics fear heretics and vice versa...both are armed; foreigners live in terror of their houses being sacked by the mob which is convinced that some, if not all foreign princes, are at the bottom of the plot. The King and Council have very prudently thought it advisable to quiet the popular feeling by issuing a proclamation in which they declare that no foreign Sovereign had any part in the conspiracy....The conduct of the French Ambassador is much criticised, not only on the ground of what I have already reported but because he would not wait for the letters the Queen was writing for France. He insisted on crossing on Monday evening though the weather was bad....He embarked three hours before the King's orders to put off his departure reached Dover and his passage was both troublesome and dangerous. They argue from this that the Ambassador, if he had not a share in the plot, at least had some knowledge of it and there is no doubt that these suspicions...may still produce a very bad effect.

Molin gives, as will be seen, a most vivid picture of the terrified James, hiding at the back of his palace for fear of experiencing a fate like his father's, and of the fear and suspicion of the mob and their intense anger against the French Catholics who were for ever accursed in English eyes on account of St Bartholomew.

Molin writes again (December 8th):

> It is quite clear that none but Catholics had a hand in the plot....On all hands one hears nothing in the mouth of the people and of the preachers except curses and insults against the Catholic religion, which, so they say, permits and approves such iniquities and inhuman actions as to blow into the air thirty thousand persons at a single stroke.

On December 22nd, Molin states that a list of all the Scots in London had been found and the general idea was that a massacre of Scots had been intended.

> Many Scots are thinking of returning home for they fear that some day a general massacre may take place....His Majesty is credited with a design to send the Prince to reside in Scotland; in this way he hopes to secure his family, for it is clear that there are many who hate not only his person but his whole race.

We can see, on the face of it, after having read such a despatch how easily the audience would perceive in Macbeth's attempt to extirpate the race of Banquo, son and father together, a parallel to the tragedy attempted in the Gunpowder Plot.

Molin also states (December 22nd) that suspicion against the French ambassador increased daily; on Tuesday, the day the mine was to have been fired, he sent a Courier with a letter in which he said: "To-day a crushing blow against the King, his house and all the nobility of England is to be delivered."

Now, in *Hamlet and the Scottish Succession*, I endeavoured to show that the main part of the material employed in *Hamlet* was really historical and that it was the historical material of most *immediate* interest to Shakespeare's audience. At the time *Hamlet* was written the subjects of most immediate interest to the Elizabethan public were the Essex conspiracy and the question of the Scottish succession. I endeavoured to show that, as Essex was supposed to have

died in his effort to bring about the Scottish succession and
to have perished as a martyr in the cause of James, the
two subjects were inseparably united in the minds of the
audience and would thus be easily made a literary unity
by the poet.

I showed that the true material of *Hamlet* was drawn not
from the so-called literary source in the *Amleth Saga* which
was really a quite different tale; but that the true material
was drawn from the history of James I and the history of
Essex. These two subjects are not a unity for us but they
were a unity for Shakespeare's audience because the tragedy
of the Essex conspiracy had bound them inseparably together and thus, throughout the play of *Hamlet*, Shakespeare
was appealing to a pre-existent unity in the minds of his
audience.

Now, something of the same kind appears to me to have
happened in the case of *Macbeth* and *King Lear*. In each
case the poet is working to a pre-existent unity in the minds
of his audience. What was the subject that filled the popular
mind and the king's mind, for Shakespeare, be it remembered, was writing especially for the Court at the time
Macbeth and *King Lear* were written?

Undoubtedly, as our contemporary documents have already been sufficient to show, undoubtedly that subject was
the Gunpowder Plot as it involved the fate of James I, of
his line, of the whole future of England.

Moreover, the plot reminded everybody, the king himself
and his people, of two of the most terrible tragedies of
history, one the Darnley murder which even modern historians have described as the most pathetic tale in the
annals of Scotland, and the other what is certainly one of
the most appalling tragedies in all the dramatic and wonderful history of France—the massacre of St Bartholomew.

I believe that Shakespeare has done in *Macbeth* almost precisely what he did in *Hamlet*; he has treated of the subjects of most *immediate* interest to his audience and he has worked to a unity pre-existent in the minds of his audience: a unity which includes the personal history of James I, especially as persecuted by the spirits of evil, who had just made in Gunpowder Plot their last and most terrible attempt to extirpate the king and his line, and which includes also the parallel cases of the Darnley murder and the massacre of St Bartholomew. All this cannot possibly be treated effectively in one drama, but some portions had been treated of in *Hamlet* (i.e. part of the Darnley tale) and other portions were to be treated of in *King Lear*.

In the case of *Hamlet* I showed, or endeavoured to show, that the so-called literary source was partly a framework and partly a disguise. Now in *Macbeth* the literary source is much more important than it was in *Hamlet*, probably for the reason that the literary source itself, i.e. the story of *Macbeth*, had (as I endeavoured to show in Chapter 1) an important and powerful bearing on the immediate situation. The story of *Macbeth*, as such, really does bear on the true subject in the poet's mind, and I find therefore that the literary source of *Macbeth* (i.e. Holinshed) is far more important than the literary source of *Hamlet* or the literary source of *King Lear*.

Now it is, of course, a commonplace that the actual story of *Macbeth* is taken from Holinshed, and from his account of the reign of Macbeth; but, as the quotation from Sir Sidney Lee[1] has already shown, the poet has introduced into the midst of the tale a narrative drawn from a quite different reign: the murder of Duff by Donwald.

Now why? Shakespeare, in this case also, is surely doing

[1] In Chap. 1.

something very curious for he is altering a story which was quite generally accepted as veracious history, and inserting into the midst of it a story from another period. We must remember that Holinshed's *Chronicle* was genuinely regarded by the Elizabethans as true and veracious history.

Try and imagine a similar parallel in a modern writer! Imagine that Browning in the midst of his *Strafford* had introduced an account of the voyage of Francis Drake, or of the battle of Blenheim. Should we not be startled by such an anachronism and enquire into its meaning?

The true explanation seems once again to lie in the mentality of the audience, and in the nature of their preoccupations at the date when *Macbeth* was written.

As the extracts quoted above have shown, the Gunpowder Plot was repeatedly compared to the Darnley murder. Now the murder of Duff by Donwald had several times been quoted by contemporary writers[1] as the nearest parallel to the Darnley murder to be found in the annals of Scotland.

In this lies, surely, a very plausible motive for its inclusion in the tale of *Macbeth*? Shakespeare's king and patron is cowering at the bottom of his palace in terror lest he should experience a fate like the fate of his father. Shakespeare has chosen a subject for a tragic drama which already has the closest relation to the subjects of his king's accession, his mission, his dynasty and the supernatural beings whom he has always regarded as his most formidable enemies. Shakespeare now modifies this subject by inserting into it another and a different story which is already admitted as the closest parallel in the annals of Scotland to the murder of the king's father.

Moreover, as I shall show later, he modifies this tale (i.e. the murder of Duff) in order to make it resemble far more

---

[1] Belleforest and Adam Blackwood.

closely than in the original the Darnley murder. Is not the motive obvious? Who could miss seeing a parallel which is, in itself, so very close and which had already been suggested more than once to the popular mind?

The Maitland Club has published a contemporary translation (1587) made by Adam Blacvod or Blackwood of a work entitled *Martyre de Marie Stuart Royne d'Escosse et Douariere de France*[1].

In this book Murray and Morton are made the villains of the story and the murder itself is compared to the murder of King Duff.

They (i.e. Murray and Morton) have well learned the deceit of Donwald, sometime Captain of the castle of Forres in Scotland, who murdered his liege lord Duffus, and punished cruelly many innocents, cruelly murdering them for the foul fact which he himself had done. But the Lord God in his mercy, who never leaveth such cruel facts unpunished...by a notable miracle made the authors of the cruel murder manifest.

We may also quote from Belleforest's *Histoire de Marie Royne d'Escosse*, 1572.

It is interesting to remember that another of Belleforest's books—*Histoires Tragiques*—either in the original or in the English translation is often supposed to have been the *immediate* source of the tale of *Hamlet*.

The passage from Belleforest which I judge the most apposite is the following:

Lisez les histoires d'Escosse, et y trouverez que Duffe roy d'Escosse fut traitreusement occis par un seigneur nommé Donwald, lequel estoit le plus aymé et caressé de son prince.... Donwald, couvant une traitresse vengeance en son ame, dissimulait accortement son maltalent et rancueur contre le roy, espiant neantmoins le temps, et l'occasion pour se prevaloir d'icelle, et venger sur le Roy....En somme ce bon roy estant logé au chasteau de Foresse (duquel ce Donwald estoit gou-

[1] Not so stated, but probably by Belleforest. See further.

verneur et capitaine) le traistre voyant le temps à propos pour executer son dessein, des que le roy fut couché, il se met à banqueter les Valetz de chambre et gardes de sa majesté et les festoya si bien jusqu'à mynuict que chargez de vins...ils s'endormirent.

Belleforest goes on to explain how Donwald with four or five of his faithful servitors enters the chamber, murders the king while his guards still sleep, carries the body away and buries it in the bed of a neighbouring river whose waters are deflected for that purpose and then allowed to return; the next morning the king's bed is found empty and covered with blood, and Donwald seizes and executes the unhappy "Valetz de chambre." Belleforest goes on to point what he thinks the close parallel with the Darnley murder:

le conte de Murray a pratiqué la mort du seigneur d'Arlay depuis faignant une pareille sainteté de justice, qu'a fait le bastard, il feit punir les innocens.

Now here we have what is admittedly the central incident of the drama of *Macbeth*, i.e. the murder of Duff by Donwald —treated as the closest possible historical parallel to the Darnley murder and inserted in the very midst of a history of Mary, Queen of Scots.

I do not for a moment believe that Shakespeare thought Murray and Morton the murderers, that was essentially the Catholic version and Shakespeare seems to me to take the Protestant version; none the less the parallel with the Donwald story had *twice* been pointed out and developed in detail by contemporary historians.

Shakespeare, in his drama, has obviously modified the details of the Donwald story; for instance the body of Duff is concealed in the bed of a river and afterwards found by miraculous means; this is told both by Holinshed and by

Belleforest. Now Shakespeare has not employed either of these incidents but, instead, he has modified the account of the murder to agree very closely with Buchanan's account of the Darnley murder.

Anyone who will compare Shakespeare's account of the murder of Duncan with Holinshed's account of the murder of Duff will see that many of the most striking incidents are not in Holinshed and have no parallel in Holinshed. The detail that the grooms are drugged so that the murder can take place without their interference and then afterwards accused of the murder belongs to the story of Duff. The story of Duff has, however, no parallel to the conference between Macbeth and Lady Macbeth alone in their chamber, it has no parallel to the striking on the bell or to the preparing of the drink; it has no parallel to the strange and dreadful silence of the night, to Macbeth's disrobing and putting on his nightgown, or of his pretence to have been awakened from sleep, it has no parallel to the knocking on the gate; but all these incidents, as I shall show, have their parallels in the Darnley murder.

But this is not all! We have seen that the Gunpowder Plot was also associated in the popular mind with the massacre of St Bartholomew, and the central incident in that massacre was the murder of Coligny.

Now these two crimes (i.e. the murder of Darnley and the murder of Coligny) had already been linked together in the closest possible relation by the Huguenot historians[1] of France who regarded them both as crimes of the Catholic League, crimes of the houses of Lorraine and Médici. It was this same Catholic League and the French branch of it in particular which were popularly considered responsible for Gunpowder Plot.

[1] *Memoires de l'estat de France sous Charles IX.*

It seems to me that Shakespeare has also drawn on the St Bartholomew massacre and the murder of Coligny for a portion of his material, especially in his account of the murder of Banquo which is quite unlike anything he found in his source.

I cannot see anything improbable in such an idea and for the following reasons:

(1) Both these crimes were magnificent and terrible dramatic material and, as a matter of fact, a number of dramatists both in Shakespeare's day and since his time have used the story of Mary Stuart and the story of St Bartholomew for dramatic purposes.

(2) The popular mind, violently excited and filled with terror by the Gunpowder Plot, was expecting every day actual living parallels to the Darnley murder and the St Bartholomew massacre.

(3) The Huguenot historians had already associated these crimes and ascribed them both to the Catholic League. The English had a particular dread of the Catholic League and of Spain for they knew that their country was the object of its special animosity.

(4) This dread of the Catholic League was well founded for it had succeeded in murdering many of the most prominent Protestants of Europe, and Henry IV of France was soon—1610—to fall a victim to Catholic fanaticism.

Shakespeare is doing in *Macbeth* what he did in *Hamlet*; he is dealing with the events of most *immediate* interest to his audience and he is working to a pre-existent unity in the minds of that audience. Events which may not seem connected to us were connected to him and to his audience because they were all vividly alive in their minds at the same moment. In *Hamlet* he worked to an emotional complex in the minds of his audience; in *Macbeth* he is working to a complex equally intense and equally living, but not the same complex; the Essex Conspiracy has faded into the background; it is now the older crimes of the Darnley murder and of the St Bartholomew massacre of which the audience has been made vividly aware; but the interests of James himself are predominant in both dramas.

CHAPTER III

MACBETH AND THE DARNLEY MURDER

As has been just pointed out, contemporary historians—Belleforest and Adam Blackwood—compared the Darnley murder to the murder of Duff by Donwald—the central incident of *Macbeth*.

I propose to point out now how close the parallels between *Macbeth* and the Darnley murder really are.

Thus the ambition of Bothwell is repeatedly dwelt on as a strongly pre-disposing motive. Robertson[1] sums it up:

> Even in that turbulent age when so many vast projects were laid open to an aspiring mind, and invited to action, no man's ambition was more daring than Bothwell's or had recourse to bolder and more singular expedients for retaining power....By complaisance and assiduity he confirmed and fortified these dispositions of the queen in his favour and insensibly paved the way towards that vast project which his ambition had perhaps already conceived, and which, in spite of so many difficulties and at the cost of so many crimes, he at last accomplished.

Now, in the murder of Duff by Donwald, the motive was not ambition but revenge; it was the revenge of a blood-feud; some of Donwald's relatives had been rebels; King Duff put them to death, and it was in order to avenge their deaths that Duff was murdered by Donwald.

Shakespeare, in his *Macbeth*, has completely altered this motive and he has substituted Bothwell's motive of

[1] *History of Scotland.*

ambition. Stress is laid on ambition as Macbeth's predominant motive throughout the play:

> thou wouldst be great,
> Art not without ambition; but without
> The illness should attend it. What thou wouldst highly,
> That wouldst thou holily[1].

In the original tale Duff was pursuing a blood-feud which gave him a kind of sanction; in *Macbeth* all the force is transferred to the more selfish motive of ambition and no mention is made of any personal injury.

Everyone has observed the irony of the passage which makes Duncan praise the delicacy of the air on his entrance into Macbeth's castle[2]; but a precisely similar irony plays a large part in Buchanan's account of the Darnley murder and occurs also in Melville's *Memoirs*.

Melville says:

> The King was afterwards brought and lodged in Kirk of Field as a place of good air where he might best recover his health; but many a one suspected that the Earl Bothwell had some enterprise against him. Few durst advertise him because he told all again to some of his own servants who were not honest.

Buchanan[3] says:

> Bothwell provided all things ready that were needful to accomplish the heinous act, first of all a house not commodious for a rich man, nor comely for a king, for it was both torn and ruinous, and had stood empty without any dweller for diverse years before.

Again the *Oration*[4] has:

> O good God! Going about to murder her husband, seeketh she for a wholesome air?...
> But let us see what manner of wholesomeness of air it is?

---

[1] I. v. [2] I. vi.
[3] *Detection of the Doings of Mary Queen of Scots.*
[4] Appended to *Detection.*

The irony, it will be observed, is precisely similar to Shakespeare's in *Macbeth*.

We might remember also that the House of Lorraine (to which Mary Queen of Scots on her mother's side belonged)[1] had a "martlet" as its badge. It is possible that Shakespeare means this bird as a piece of symbolism which intensifies and deepens the irony.

DUN. This castle hath a pleasant seat; the air
    Nimbly and sweetly recommends itself
    Unto our gentle senses.

BAN.   This guest of summer,
    The temple-haunting martlet, does approve,
    By his lov'd mansionry, that the heaven's breath
    Smells wooingly here;...
    Where they most breed and haunt, I have observ'd,
    The air is delicate[2].

There is, of course, no mention of "wholesome air" in Holinshed's story; it is one of those profound tragic ironies which Shakespeare introduces himself and it is exactly like the tragic irony of the "wholesome air" in Buchanan's account of the Darnley murder. As Melville's mention of it in his *Memoirs* also serves to show, it had deeply impressed the imagination of the time.

The murder takes place by night and it is notable that the Scottish proclamations dwell particularly on the depth of the night, its deadness and the intensity of its silence, and the solitariness of the victim. They speak of the crime as "The horrible and unworthy murder of the King, our Sovereign's late father, committed under silence of night within his own lodging by James, Earl of Bothwell[3]." This is only one example, but I could quote many more; the

---

[1] The Cardinal of Lorraine was supposed to have instigated the Darnley murder.   [2] I. vi.
[3] *Register of the Privy Council of Scotland*, July 9th, 1567.

phrase "under silence of night" is, in fact, repeated like a refrain in nearly all the proclamations: it was, again, one of the details that impressed contemporaries most.

So in *Macbeth* the silence of the night is made particularly and horribly prominent. It is one of the details we are never allowed to forget[1].

> Didst thou not hear a noise?

Macbeth asks and is answered:

> I heard the owl scream, and the crickets cry,

and in his own soliloquy he speaks of the intense deadness of the night:

> Now o'er the one half-world
> Nature seems dead.

Lady Macbeth, listening in an agony of apprehension, hears nothing but the screaming of the owl.

Before the murder took place there occurred, according to Buchanan and others, a conversation between Mary and Bothwell in her chamber. Buchanan says[2]:

After that she was come into her chamber, after midnight, she was in long talk with Bothwell, none being present but the captain of her guard. And when he also withdrew himself, Bothwell was there left alone, without other company, and shortly after retired into his own chamber.

Now, as I have pointed out before, there is no mention of any such colloquy in Holinshed, either in the Macbeth tale or in the murder of Duff, yet, as everyone will agree, it is one of the most tragic and terrible scenes in Shakespeare. The leading motive is surely to be found in the passage from Buchanan I have quoted[3].

Another important point may be observed here. As I have said, Shakespeare sweeps away the blood-feuds which

---

[1] II. i, ii.   [2] *Detection.*   [3] See also Chap. VII.

are so prominent in Holinshed; Duff is inspired by such blood-feuds and so is Holinshed's Lady Macbeth; Holinshed's Lady Macbeth is also inspired by personal ambition:

speciallie his wife lay sore upon him to attempt the thing, as she that was verie ambitious, burning in unquenchable desire to bear the name of a queen.

Shakespeare sweeps away this motive also and substitutes Lady Macbeth's ambition for her husband. Now this is a much more unselfish motive and it certainly does resemble the history, for Bothwell had, as Robertson has shown, an insatiable ambition and Mary did particularly desire to gratify it.

The murder takes place while the victim is in his bed; it thus combines the maximum of meanness in the crime with the maximum of helplessness in the victim.

Now in the case of Darnley it was precisely this peculiar combination of circumstances, the murder of a helpless, sleeping man in his own bed, which most horrified contemporaries, as we can see by scores of references in the proclamations and elsewhere[1]. Nor was this all! Two sleeping servants had been killed with the king and this was rightly regarded as a dreadful exaggeration of the horrible deed. Thus Pitcairn[2] recounts that on March 25th, 1567, the prisoners were accused of

the shameful, treasonable and abominable slaughter and murder of the late King's grace, father to our sovereign lord, in his own lodging for the time...where he was lying in his bed, taking the night's rest...also for the cruel slaughter and murder of the late William Taylor, his grace's servitor, and the late Andrew Macaig treasonably...under silence of the night.

[1] *Register of the Privy Council of Scotland*, 1567.
[2] *Ancient Scottish Criminal Trials.*

We may also compare the contemporary poem, the *Legend of Mary, Queen of Scotland*[1]:

> A traitorous death by train of powder laid
> Whilst he in bed his heedless bones did reste,
>
>   *   *   *   *   *   *
>
> In dead of night, a time for treason's best,
> When he and his with sleep were now opprest;
> Then was his life bereft.

The *Oration* lays stress on the same fact, "they kept the keys of the upper room that the murderers might come to the King in his bed."

It is notable that in *Macbeth* there is mention of a drink for Macbeth immediately before the murder takes place:

> Go bid thy mistress, when my drink is ready,
> She strike upon the bell[2].

So we read in the testimony of George Dalgleish[3]:

> So soon as my lord came to his lodging he cried for a drink and incontinent thereafter took off his clothes and went to his bed and lay there by the space of half-an-hour or thereby.

So Macbeth returns to his bed after the murder and then pretends to be aroused from sleep. Lady Macbeth says:

> Get on your nightgown, lest occasion call us,
> And show us to be watchers.

Then when Macduff asks: "Is thy master stirring?" he answers his own question by saying:

> Our knocking has awaked him; here he comes.

The drama exactly resembles the Darnley murder where Dalgleish deposed: "Hacket came to him (i.e. Bothwell) in great fright; and incontinent my lord rose and put on his clothes...and...departed forth of the chamber."

---

[1] Attributed to Wenman.   [2] II. i.   [3] Pitcairn.

No mention is made in Holinshed of a drink being ready, or of the murderer returning to bed and pretending to sleep, or of his being roused.

The terrible incident of the knocking at the door, making such a clamour in the night, which is justly regarded as having such an appalling effect in the tragedy, simply does not occur in the literary source at all; but it occurs twice over in the Darnley murder, once when Bothwell knocked with a clamour which roused people on the gate of the Kirk in the Field, leading to poor Darnley, and once when his servant roused him.

The door on which the knocking took place is prominently shown in the Record Office contemporary design of the Darnley murder[1].

In *Macbeth* there are two servants who lie in a room a little apart. Macbeth says:

> There 's one did laugh in 's sleep, and one cried "Murder!"
> That they did wake each other: I stood and heard them:
> But they did say their prayers, and address'd them
> Again to sleep[2].

Lady Macbeth answers:

> There are two lodg'd together.

So in Nelson's deposition[3] we read: "he lay with Edward Symons in the little gallery, that went direct to the South out of the king's chamber."

The two lodged apart are, be it observed, quite different servants from the two murdered with Duncan, for the latter are in the king's bedchamber.

The parallel with the Darnley murder is curiously exact, for in the Darnley story two servants were killed with the king and the two lodged apart survived to give evidence.

---

[1] Museum of the Record Office.   [2] II. ii.   [3] Pitcairn.

Hepburn's deposition[1] is also exceedingly interesting as a commentary upon this part of *Macbeth*:

> Bothwell, on coming in, immediately called for a drink, and taking off his clothes went to bed in which he remained about half-an-hour, when a messenger came to the gate, knocking, and was admitted.
>
> "What is the matter?" said Bothwell to him.
>
> "The King's house," he answered, "is blown up and I trow the King is slain."
>
> "Fie! Treason!" cried out Bothwell; and then he rose and put on his clothes. Thereafter the Earl of Huntley and many others came to him and they went to the queen's chamber.

Here we surely have the closest parallels with Macbeth; the drink, the taking off of the clothes, the pretence of sleep, the knocking at the door, the cry of "Treason!"

In the drama it is Macduff who first cries "Treason!"; but Macbeth, exactly like Bothwell, pretends the utmost concern and horror.

In the drama we have Macbeth's statement that none will dare to impugn the deed because the doers have all the power. Macbeth asks[2]:

> Will it not be received,
> When we have mark'd with blood those sleepy two
> Of his own chamber and used their very daggers,
> That they have done 't?

And Lady Macbeth answers:

> Who dares receive it other,
> As we shall make our griefs and clamour roar
> Upon his death?

This impudence and audacity were exactly paralleled in the Darnley trial; thus we read in the confession of the Laird of Ormistown that Bothwell said to him: "none dare find fault with it when it shall be done."

[1] Pitcairn.   [2] I. vii.

The heavy sense that no one dared speak for justice was the burden that weighed upon all men's minds in the Darnley murder. We read in the *Spanish State Papers*, April 21st, 1567:

the trial took place on the day appointed, namely, the 12th, and no accuser or witness appeared against the Earl, who was acquitted by the majority of the judges, who were ordered by the Queen to declare their judgment; but the rest of them would not vote as they considered the trial was not free, the Earl of Bothwell having large forces with him and Lennox being ordered to bring not more than six horsemen. For this reason there was no one to bring or support the charge.

It was, of course, the Earl of Lennox, the king's father, who was the chief accuser and it is notable that one of the chief accusers in *Macbeth* is made a Lennox[1].

> My former speeches have but hit your thoughts,
> Which can interpret further: only, I say,
> Things have been strangely borne. The gracious Duncan
> Was pitied of Macbeth:—marry, he was dead:—
> And the right-valiant Banquo walk'd too late;
> Whom, you may say, if 't please you, Fleance kill'd,
> For Fleance fled: men must not walk too late.
> Who cannot want the thought how monstrous
> It was for Malcolm and for Donalbain
> To kill their gracious father? damned fact!
> How it did grieve Macbeth! did he not straight
> In pious rage the two delinquents tear,
> That were the slaves of drink, and thralls of sleep?
> Was not that nobly done? Ay, and wisely too;
> For 'twould have angered any heart alive
> To hear the men deny 't.

This is almost exactly the attitude of Lennox in the actual history of the Darnley case; he was the chief accuser, but he dared not speak openly because the Court was packed with Bothwell's adherents and Lennox's

[1] II. iii; III. vi.

own men had been expressly limited in numbers. The Lennox in the play also ardently desires help from England and so did the actual Lennox of history. The bitter irony and the powerlessness are the same both in the history and in the drama.

Now in Holinshed there is no mention of any Lennox who is an accuser, and why should Shakespeare introduce this person and bring him prominently forward unless he is deliberately pointing the way to the Darnley murder?

As an example of the manner in which enquiry was suppressed we may recall the letter which Kirkaldy of Grange wrote to the Earl of Bedford:

> She (i.e. Mary) is so past all shame that she has caused make an Act of Parliament against all them that shall set up any writing that shall speak anything of him (i.e. Bothwell) [1].

We read the same thing in a list of Memoranda by Cecil intended as instructions for Lord Grey, April 25th, 1567.

> The messenger is to inform her (i.e. Mary) that the Queen daily finds from all parts a general misliking conceived that as yet no discovery is made of the malefactors, but that which is most misliked is that they are such as by common fame have been most favoured.

The hallucination of the dagger plays an important part in *Macbeth*.

It seems to me more than probable that it was suggested by the illustrations of the Darnley murder which were current at the time. Thus in the *Calendar of Scottish State Papers* there is an Allegorical Sketch in colour which represents the queen, naked to the waist, as a mermaid.

> Below within a circle surrounded by 17 swords or daggers, points outwards a hare or rabbit I H above. Indorsed (by Drury) the people's applying of this I H is for Bodevill, John Hepborne. There was also a rude copy of the same with mottoes: "Spe illecto inani, Timor undique clades."

[1] *State Papers*, Foreign Series.

If one desired a motto for Macbeth one could hardly find a better one than this; he certainly did find his hope vain and himself surrounded by fear and slaughter.

There is also a contemporary plan of the Darnley murder, already alluded to, which is preserved in the Record Office[1], and which shows different stages of the murder. In one of these stages the bodies of the king and his servant are shown and above them, represented as if floating in the air, is a dagger.

We may compare this with what Drury says of Bothwell after the murder[2]:

His followers to the number of fifty follow him very near, their gesture as his is much noted. His hand, as he talks to any that is not assured to him upon his dagger with a strange countenance.

Three such examples are sufficient to show that contemporary opinion regarded the dagger, pre-eminently the weapon of the assassin, as in some sort a symbol of Bothwell.

Mr Hubert Hall informs me that contemporary documents, of one kind or another, were copied very freely and passed from hand to hand. I think it more than probable that the famous dagger hallucination in *Macbeth* was suggested by the design preserved in the Record Office (or some variant of it) with the assassin's dagger floating in the air; a further confirmation of this is suggested by the fact that another compartment contains a picture of a very heavily barred postern, representing the Kirk of the Field's portal, Bothwell's knocking on which caused such an outcry[3].

A third compartment contains a picture of a child with the inscription: "Judge and avenge my cause, O Lord!" a broken branch lying by the dead bodies.

[1] Also in Print Room of British Museum.
[2] Quoted by Hay Fleming.   [3] Pitcairn.

This corresponds very closely to a later scene in *Macbeth*[1], it resembles one of the avenging figures shown to Macbeth by the witches, namely, the third apparition: a child crowned with a tree in his hand. Macbeth enquires:

> What is this
> That rises like the issue of a king,
> And wears upon his baby-brow the round
> And top of sovereignty?

Now none of these three things are found in Shakespeare's literary source; Holinshed has no mention of a dagger, no barred portal, no reference whatever to a child crowned and holding the broken branch of a tree, and I find it quite incredible that all three resemblances can have come by accident; we find the dagger in the air pointing the way towards the murdered bodies, just as in *Macbeth* it points the way towards Duncan; in some of the designs we find it flecked with blood; there is also the prominent position given to the barred portal, the knocking on which played such an important part in the murder and which suggests the gate and the knocking on the gate in *Macbeth*, and there is the child who is crowned, obviously typifying the infant king, with the broken branch which typifies either the tree under which Darnley's body was found or the broken branch of Darnley's life or, more probably, both together.

Such designs played a prominent part at the time, for one of them was used on the banner of the Confederate Lords[2].

I must repeat that I think the Record Office design, or some variant of it, an important source for *Macbeth*; it makes very prominent the dagger in the air, the barred portal and the child crowned, all of which play such an important part in *Macbeth* and *none of which* are found in Holinshed.

[1] IV. i.   [2] See *Hamlet and the Scottish Succession*.

All three also illustrate what I said in the Introduction, that the mentality of the time very naturally and very easily turned history into symbolism.

I really cannot imagine how closer parallels could be dramatised and put on the stage.

We may observe that the Scottish Act of Parliament deposing Mary accuses her of a similar part in the deed to that of Lady Macbeth and a similar dissimulation:

she was privy, airt and pairt of the actual desire and deed of the foresaid murder of the King...our said sovereign lord's mother with the said James, sometime Earl of Bothwell, went about by indirect and coloured means to colour and hold back the knowledge of the truth of the committers of the said crime.

Exactly as in *Macbeth*, however, the real truth was suspected.

The Act continues:

Yet all men in their hearts were fully persuaded, of the authors and devisers of that mischievous and unworthy fact, awaiting while God should move the hearts of some to enter on the quarrel for revenging of the same....

Now, I have already pointed out that in Shakespeare's literary source, i.e. Holinshed, there is not this *immediate* anger against Macbeth because Macbeth reigns excellently, and with the full consent of his subjects, for the greater part of his seventeen years reign.

Here again Shakespeare departs from his literary source and closely resembles the history.

Another peculiar phrase that is repeatedly employed in the Darnley murder is the phrase as to the "cleansing" of Bothwell which, again, is a parallel with Macbeth.

> Go get some water,
> And wash this filthy witness from your hand[1],

[1] II. ii.

and again:

> Will all great Neptune's ocean wash this blood
> Clean from my hand?

and

> A little water clears us of this deed.

The contemporary parallels run[1] April 13th, 1567:

> James Earl Bothwell has set up a writing subscribed with his hand that he was "cleansed" of the king's murder.

On April 20th Kirkaldy of Grange writes to Bedford "that the Queen caused ratify in Parliament the cleansing of Bothwell." No such word is used in Holinshed nor is there a reference to any such ceremony.

The disgrace of the unpunished murder is dwelt upon both in the play and in the contemporary records.

Thus the *Spanish State Papers*[2] say of Murray:

> The Earl...arrived here....He said he did not intend to return until the Queen had punished the persons concerned in her husband's death, as he thought it was unworthy of his position to remain in a country where so strange and extraordinary a crime went unpunished.

On March 8th Killigrew writes to Cecil[3]:

> I see...a general misliking among the Commons, and some others who abhor the detestable murder of their King, a shame as they suppose to the whole nation.

The fame of it is dispersed through the whole world as a disgrace. We read in Cecil's Memoranda of April 25th instructions for messages that "the Queen of Scots may understand what manner of bruits and rumours are spread through all countries concerning the said fact" (i.e. the king's murder). Melville says in his *Memoirs*:

---

[1] *Calendar of Scottish State Papers.*
[2] Simancas *Archives.*   [3] *State Papers*, Foreign Series.

All Scotland cried out upon the foul murder of the King. But few of them were careful how to get it revenged, till they were driven thereto, by the crying out of all other nations generally against Scottishmen, wherever they travelled either by sea or by land.

There is also a letter from the Scottish lords to the king of France:

Votre Majeste nous a remonte ceste promesse, nous mettant devant les yeux la grande hunt que ce nous seroit à jamois, si un faict si enorme, perpetre en la persone du roy, demeurast casche. Ceste remonstrance, joincte avec tant d'advertisse-ments que nous recevons de jour a autre, des Escossois qui sont espars par les pays estrangers, nous a servy d'esperon pour nous faire enterprendre lenquest dudict meurtre, qui par trop a este differe, de sorte que toute ceste nation en est aucune-ment dishonore. Len la nous mande de tous cestes que les Escossois, tant en France qu'allieurs, se sentent tant inter-ressees, oyans taxer toute la nation que pour honte ils n'osent montre le visage; ains sont contraincts quasi de desadvouer leur patrie, voyants la nonchallance ou connivence de ceux a qui le faict touchoit le plus.

The *Register of the Privy Council of Scotland* repeatedly contains proclamations to the same effect:

it behoved them (i.e. the lords) to take arms to punish and revenge the said shameful murder wherewith this whole realm and lieges thereof were slandered and defamed.

Again in 1567 we have the Bond of the Scottish Nobles[1]:

Since the horrible murder of the King, the Queen's Majesty's husband, is so odious not only before God, but also to the whole world, with continual infamy and shame to this realm if this same murder shall not be punished accordingly...the plague of God shall not depart from the country or town where innocent blood is shed, before the same shall be cleansed by shedding the blood of the offenders.

[1] *Calendar of Scottish State Papers.*

Again on March 10th we have news from France[1]:

> On the 23rd there arrived one by whom they understood all
> the manner of the Scottish King's death. It astonished the
> King here so that counsel was given that the Scottish guard
> should be cassed for a suspicion conceived by the deed of the
> nation's infidelity.

We see from the above extracts that there is the clearest
contemporary evidence to the effect that the murder of
James' father was considered as having disgraced Scotland
in the eyes of all Europe and that it gave the Scots a bad
reputation everywhere and even caused the disbanding of
the Scottish guard in France.

Now this is the situation that is dwelt upon with such
burning passion in *Macbeth*.

In the mouth of Macbeth himself we have an anticipation
of the unutterable infamy that will accompany his deed[2]:

> pity, like a naked new-born babe,
> Striding the blast, or heaven's cherubim, horsed
> Upon the sightless couriers of the air,
> Shall blow the horrid deed in every eye,
> That tears shall drown the wind.

The metaphor of "pity like a naked new-born babe" seems
suggested by James himself, since pity for the infant prince
certainly was a main motive urged against the criminals, and
the infant prince appealing to heaven for justice plays a
prominent part in contemporary pictures, i.e. that on the
banner of the Confederate Lords, in the Record Office print
already alluded to etc., etc.; the sweeping of the "horrid
deed" abroad on the air is almost exactly the language of
the proclamations.

One curious point may be considered here.

As we have seen, the night of the murder is described as
being intensely still; but, when the night is described after-

---

[1] *State Papers*, Foreign Series.   [2] I. vii.

wards, we are told that it has been tempestuous almost
beyond human memory.

On the one hand we have the absolute stillness:

> Now o'er the one half-world
> Nature seems dead, and wicked dreams abuse
> The curtain'd sleep[1].

And Lady Macbeth's:

> I heard the owl scream, and the crickets cry.

It is impossible to imagine a stillness more deep.

And yet this night has also seen a tempest without
parallel. Lennox says[2]:

> The night has been unruly; where we lay,
> Our chimneys were blown down; and, as they say,
> Lamentings heard i' the air; strange screams of death,
> And prophesying with accents terrible
> Of dire combustion and confus'd events
> *   *   *   some say the earth
> Was feverous, and did shake.

Now surely it is strange how a night so intensely still that
Lady Macbeth hears only the owls and the crickets and that
Macbeth feels the whole world dead, surely it is strange how
a night so calm should also be the night of a terrific tempest
when chimneys are blown down and the night of an earthquake? Macbeth admits:

> 'twas a rough night,

and Lennox answers:

> My young remembrance cannot parallel
> A fellow to it.

A contradiction so acute seems to me only explicable on
the ground that Shakespeare is really writing symbolism:
the "silence of the night" really is the silence of the night

---

[1] II. i.   [2] II. iii.

which surrounds the murder of the unhappy king of Scotland, referred to with horror in proclamation after proclamation: "the horrible and unworthy murder of the King...committed under silence of the night within his own lodging[1]."

On the other hand, the dreadful tempest which carries the news to every land seems to me to be just as plainly the disgrace of it as published to the whole world or as the Articles of the Kirk (July 25th, 1567) put it "with continual infamy and shame to this realm if this same murder shall not be punished accordingly."

It is worthy of note that *neither* the silence of the night *nor* the tempest occur in Holinshed who refers neither to the one nor the other; certain dread phenomena do occur in the murder of Duff but not these.

The passage about the earth being feverous and shaking is another that seems to refer quite obviously to the Darnley murder, for the explosion of the gunpowder was referred to several times in the trial as making the ground shake like an earthquake and also making a similar noise.

[1] July 9th, 1567, July 21st, 1567, etc., etc.

CHAPTER IV

MACBETH AND THE DARNLEY MURDER (*cont.*)

In addition to the immediate details of the Darnley murder there are also other portions of *Macbeth* which appear to have been suggested by the elder Bothwell.

Thus we have the accusations of lechery which are so repeatedly brought against Bothwell:

"He was brought up," says the author of the *Oration*, "in the Bishop of Murray's palace...in drunkenness and whoredomes, amongst most vile ministers of dissolute misorder."

"After that he was grown to man's estate at dice and among harlots he wasted a most goodly revenue of his inheritance... he defiled other men's houses with cuckolddome....As for excessive and immoderate use of lechery, he therein no less sought to be famous than other men do shun dishonour and infamy."

Compare what is said of Macbeth[1]:

> I grant him bloody,
> Luxurious, avaricious, false, deceitful,
> Sudden, malicious, smacking of every sin
> That has a name.

We have no parallel in Holinshed for the lechery; his Macbeth reigns admirably for ten years and then, his conscience pricking him, becomes a bloody tyrant; but he is not accused of lechery. Also we may observe he does for ten years rule far better than Duncan ever did, as is generally acknowledged, and passes excellent laws.

Shakespeare's Macbeth, after the murder is once committed, never shows any virtues and never possesses an hour of ease; this corresponds very closely to the actual

---

[1] IV. iii.

history where Bothwell was at once suspected and had no interval of contentment or of good reputation.

Macbeth is repeatedly called a "bloody tyrant" and so is Bothwell. Thus we have in the *State Papers*, July 21st, 1567, concerning Bothwell:

No counsellors of the realm had liberty of free speech or surety of their own life if they should in council resist the inordinate affections of that bloody tyrant.

Compare this with Macbeth[1]:

> O nation miserable,
> With an untitled tyrant bloody-scepter'd,

and also[2]

> There's not a one of them but in his house
> I keep a servant fee'd,

which shows a similar grip over the nobles.

Both Bothwell and Macbeth are stated to have broken men for servants: the Memoranda of Cecil, April 25th[3] state:

It is commonly said that the Earl of Bothwell was the principal author of the King's death...and that Bothwell's servitors, being broken men, were the cause of it.

"Bothwell's servants," says Buchanan in the *Detection*, "were robbers, pirates and thieves."

We may compare this with the scene where Macbeth instructs the murderers of Banquo, the Second Murderer says[4]:

> I am one, my liege,
> Whom the vile blows and buffets of the world
> Have so incens'd that I am reckless what
> I do to spite the world.

and the First Murderer responds:

> And I another,
> So weary with disasters, tugg'd with fortune,
> That I would set my life on any chance,
> To mend it, or be rid on 't.

[1] IV. iii.   [2] III. iv.   [3] *State Papers*, Foreign Series.   [4] III. i.

It is sufficiently obvious from this that Macbeth's followers are broken men and outlaws.

These references to broken men and outlaws certainly do not occur in Holinshed. We may remember in this connection that the historic Bothwell was accused of piracy, and on this charge was imprisoned in Denmark for ten years before his death.

Again Bothwell's servants, when they were not "broken men," were usually unwilling and, in the conflict with the Scottish lords, they had not their hearts in the fight. Melville states in his *Memoirs*: "The Earl Bothwell convened a great number but they came unwillingly"; "so many as came had no hearts to fight in that quarrel"; and again "Part of his own company detested him."

We have exactly similar circumstances in Shakespeare's *Macbeth*[1]:

> Both more and less have given him the revolt;
> And none serve with him but constrainèd things,
> Whose hearts are absent too,

and again:

> This way, my lord; the castle's gently render'd:
> The tyrant's people on both sides do fight[2].

Another interesting correspondence lies between Bothwell's hesitation to join in single combat and Macbeth's similar hesitation.

On April 13th, 1567, we have a proclamation:

The Earl of Bothwell having offered to fight according to the law of arms any gentleman undefamed who dares to say that he is not innocent...the writer offers to prove by the same law of arms that he was the chief and author of the foul and horrible murder[3].

[1] v. iv.   [2] v. vii.   [3] *State Papers*, Foreign Series.

This challenge was not accepted. Buchanan also notes Bothwell's unfulfilled offer of single combat:

> A notice was put up that...though Bothwell had been lawfully cleansed of the murder...he was ready to try it in combat; if any man of good fame and a gentleman born would charge him with the murder of the king.

The *Oration* makes it a bitter taunt against Bothwell that he refused:

> And when there were many on the other side of honorable birth and estates, that offered to accept the combat, by and by his violent heat cooled and his glorious speech failed.

We may compare this with the scene in *Macbeth*[1]; Macbeth is willing to fight Macduff if he really has a charm against him; but, when he finds the charm does not hold, he declines:

> I'll not fight with thee.

and has to be taunted by Macduff:

> Then yield thee, coward,
> And live to be the show and gaze o' the time:
> We'll have thee, as our rarer monsters are,
> Painted upon a pole, and underwrit,
> "Here may you see the tyrant."

It is only by such taunts that Macbeth can be goaded to fight; his failure of courage in such a crucial moment has been blamed by some commentators as improbable; but it is the feeling of Macbeth's guilt which unnerves his arm, and probably in the history also it was the feeling of guilt which unnerved Bothwell and made a man naturally courageous behave in one case like a coward. There is no parallel to this refusal of the single combat in Holinshed; Macbeth and Macduff fight but Macbeth does not hesitate.

[1] v. viii.

Bothwell, we may also observe, was repeatedly accused of witchcraft:

> On Feb. 16th, the morning after Darnley's funeral, an anonymous placard was found affixed to the door of the Tolbooth charging the Earl of Bothwell, Sir James Balfour etc....with the murder of the king and that the queen was assenting thereto, through the persuasion of the Earl of Bothwell, and the witchcraft of the Lady Buccleugh[1].

We have also an interesting account of the way in which such matters were put into contemporary dramas:

> On May 14th, 1567, Drury writes to Cecil: "There has been an interlude of boys at Stirling of the manner of the King's death and the arraignment of the earl....This was before the Lords, who the Earl thinks were devisers of the same....It is thought that the witches and sorcerers have some credit for the appointment of the time of the marriage[2]."

Another striking parallel between the history and the play is to be found in the melancholy and sickness of the queen.

On March 29th, 1567, Sir William Drury wrote to Cecil:

> the judgment of the people is that the queen will marry Bothwell. The Cardinal seems to mislike with her for the death of the King. She has been for the most part either melancholy or sickly ever since.

Again on March 30th, Drury writes: "The Queen of Scots was troubled with some sickness, of which she is not yet all free[3]." Later on this melancholy developed into a desire for suicide: "Alone with Bothwell she was heard," says de Croc, "to call for a knife to slay herself[4]." "Only two days after the wedding," say the *Spanish State Papers*, "she cried for a knife that she might kill herself." De Silva was inclined to

---

[1] *State Papers*, Foreign Series.
[2] *State Papers*, Foreign Series. Cp. also *Hamlet and the Scottish Succession*.
[3] *State Papers*, Foreign Series.
[4] Quoted by Andrew Lang.

explain her misery by the maxim that "an evil conscience can know no peace."

Even before Darnley's death we find that Mary had been supposed to have the falling sickness (i.e. epilepsy).

Also on May 20th, 1567, Drury writes to Cecil: "It is thought the Queen has long had a spice of the falling sickness, and has been of late troubled therewith."

Now here we surely have remarkable parallels with *Macbeth*. The queen has been full of resolution before the murder; but, afterwards, she falls into melancholy, she is suspected of the desire for suicide and she is subject to strange trances in one of which she walks and talks in her sleep.

Macbeth speaks of[1]:

> the affliction of these terrible dreams
> That shake us nightly:

implying that his wife, like himself, suffers torments of conscience. There is no doubt of the terrible melancholy of her last hours. Macbeth enquires[2]:

> How does your patient, doctor?

and is answered:

> Not so sick, my lord,
> As she is troubled with thick-coming fancies,
> That keep her from her rest.

He replies:

> Cure her of that.
> Canst thou not minister to a mind diseas'd;
> Pluck from the memory a rooted sorrow,
> Raze out the written troubles of the brain;
> And, with some sweet oblivious antidote,
> Cleanse the stuff'd bosom of that perilous stuff
> Which weighs upon the heart?

[1] III. ii.   [2] V. iii.

Suicide is repeatedly suggested as a possibility[1]:

> Look after her;
> Remove from her the means of all annoyance,
> And still keep eyes upon her,

and[2]   this dead butcher, and his fiend-like queen,
> Who, as 'tis thought, by self and violent hands
> Took off her life.

It seems to me more than probable that the wonderful and terrible scene of the sleep-walking was suggested by the idea of the epileptic trance; at any rate such phenomena are of frequent occurrence in epilepsy and closely associated with it. Here, as in the case of Bothwell's dagger, a historical parallel may well have been used by Shakespeare as a starting-point and have been elaborated by him into one of the most wonderful efforts of his imaginative genius.

We note, as before, that none of these things occur in Shakespeare's literary source. Holinshed has no mention of the queen's melancholy or remorse, he says nothing of any desire for suicide, he has no reference to sleep-walking nor to anything whatever which might serve as a starting-point.

If Shakespeare really wished to dramatise history it is difficult to see how he could dramatise it better and more effectively.

I propose to refer now to Holinshed's account of the murder of Duff by Donwald in order that the reader may compare it in detail with *Macbeth* and realise how much in the play is due to historical sources.

Holinshed dates the event 968.

He speaks of the king—Duff—being vexed by a strange sickness which was "no natural sickness, but by sorcerie and magicall art, practised by a sort of witches dwelling in a house of Mury land, called Fores."

[1] v. i.   [2] v. viii.

Donwald, lieutenant of Forres, discovers the witches and has them put to death by fire. The king—Duff—thereupon recovers; he chases the rebels into Rosse and from Rosse into Caithness. He also puts to death some of the rebels who are relatives of Donwald's; this enrages the latter. Donwald's wife also has cause for anger against the king and persuades her husband to make away with him.

I shall deal in the next chapter with the witch motive in *Macbeth*; here I only wish o point out that there are several important motives in the murder of Duff by Donwald which differ greatly from Shakespeare's dramatic version; the king himself is a victim of art-magic, but that is a motive omitted by Shakespeare, who says nothing of the king pining away, nor does he say anything of the death of the witches by fire.

Also, as we have pointed out before, the motive ascribed to Donwald and his wife is different; it is neither ambition on the husband's part nor wifely devotion on the wife's; in each case it is one of those blood-feuds or revenges for the murders of kinsmen which played such a large part in mediaeval history. Holinshed's Lady Macbeth had also a similar motive. Shakespeare drops out altogether these blood-feuds which give a sort of wild justice even to the crimes of Donwald and Lady Macbeth. He substitutes the more purely egoistic motives of ambition on the one side and personal affection on the other which exactly correspond to the motives of the history.

To resume Holinshed's account of the murder:

Donwald, thus being the more kindled in wrath by the words of his wife, determined to follow her advice in the execution of so heinous an act. Whereupon devising with himself for a while, which way he might best accomplish his cursed intent, at length got opportunitie and sped his purpose as followeth. It chanced that the king upon the daie before he purposed to depart forth of the castell, was long in his oratory at his prayers, and there continued till it was late in the night. At the last, comming forth, he called such afore him as had faithfully served him in pursuit and apprehension of the rebels, and giving them hearty thanks, he bestowed sundry honourable gifts among them....

At length, having talked with them a long time, he got him into his privie chamber, onelie with two of his chamberlains, who having brought him to bed, came forth again and then fell to banqueting with Donwald and his wife who had prepared diverse delicate dishes, and sundry sorts of drinks for their rear supper or collation, whereat they sat up so long...that their heads were no sooner got to the pillow, but asleep they were so fast, that a man might have removed the chamber over them, sooner than to have awaked them out of their drunken sleep.

Then Donwald, though he abhorred the act greatly in heart, yet through the instigation of his wife he called four of his servants unto him...they gladly obeyed his instructions and speedily going about the murder, they enter the chamber (in which the king lay) a little before cockcrow where they secretly cut his throat as he lay sleeping without any bustling at all and immediately by a postern gate they carried forth the dead body into the fields....

Holinshed goes on to narrate how the murderers deflected a small river, dug a hole in the bed of the stream, buried the body in the hole and then returned the stream to its course, so that the body might not betray Donwald by bleeding in his presence.

Donwald slew the chamberlains as guilty of that heinous murder, and then like a madman running to and fro, he ransacked every corner within the castle...he burdened the chamberlains, whom he had slain, with all the fault, they having the keys of the castle committed to their keeping all the night.

Now here we have at once important parallels and important differences.

In the first place we observe that, as both Belleforest and Adam Blackwood had in Shakespeare's own day pointed out, there were close parallels between the Duff murder and the Darnley murder and therefore a large part of *Macbeth* is itself parallel with both.

Similar in each case is the friendship between the victim and the murderers, the misplaced confidence of the victim who puts himself in the power of the murderers, the murder at night and in the bed, the murder of the two servants, the ascribing of the guilt to the innocent, and the murderer's pretended concern and pretended vengeance.

We may observe here that, in Duff's murder, Donwald apparently contents himself with putting the guilt on the two grooms; but, in the Darnley murder, the real accusations were, of course, laid by the Scottish lords against each other, and Shakespeare makes the suggested motive the suborning of the grooms by the king's sons—a motive not one whit more fantastic than the actual accusations brought in the history.

The story of the disposal of the body of Donwald has no parallel in *Macbeth*, for Shakespeare omits it wholly. On the other hand he has made the parallel to the history much more close by introducing a number of motives which are not in Holinshed at all, but which are found in the history: ambition instead of revenge as the real cause of the murder, the passionate devotion of the woman to the man's ambition, the intense silence of the night, the conversation between the guilty pair in the chamber, the preparation of the drink, the wonderful motive of the dagger, the retiring to bed and pretending to be asleep, the wonderful motive of the knocking in the middle of the night, the curious detail of the tempest which is somehow simultaneous with a night of perfect calm, the use of the name of Lennox as one of the chief accusers, the detail that the "earth was feverous and did shake," the fact that Macbeth was licentious, that broken men and outlaws were his servants, that he tried to evade a challenge to single combat, that he was accused of witchcraft; all these make a formidable list of motives which are not in Holinshed, but are in the history; we have others connected with the queen, her bitter remorse, her desire to commit suicide, her strange trances.

Moreover in contemporary pictorial representations can be found three of the leading effects in *Macbeth*, the dagger floating in the air, the barred door on which the knocking takes place, and the child crowned and with a branch.

When we remember that the murder of Duff had been already singled out by two of Shakespeare's contemporaries as the nearest parallel in Scottish history to the Darnley murder—it surely becomes sufficiently obvious what Shakespeare is doing; he takes the story which is the nearest possible parallel to the Darnley murder and then makes it more like by employing material which corresponds very closely to the actual details of the murder. It is the method which Hamlet employs in the Gonzago play; he chooses a story closely resembling the story of his father's murder and then makes the resemblance more close; it is the method which, I believe, Shakespeare himself employs in *Hamlet*[1].

He employs it again in *Macbeth*.

This is, I take it, the main reason for the inclusion of the murder of Duff by Donwald in an alien reign.

[1] See *Hamlet and the Scottish Succession.*

CHAPTER V

MACBETH AND FRANCIS, EARL BOTHWELL

In *Hamlet and the Scottish Succession* I showed how Shakespeare had combined together the elder and the younger Bothwell into the one figure of Claudius; he was attempting to dramatise Scottish History and it did not admit of dramatisation without condensation and compression. The figure of James I himself was, of all others, the figure most likely to interest his, i.e. Shakespeare's, audience; the crime of his father's murder was an extraordinarily dramatic crime, lending itself readily to treatment on the stage; so were James' own personal relations to the younger Bothwell extraordinarily interesting; the two subjects made, however, infinitely better material if united in one drama and hence, I maintained, Shakespeare had united in one the parts of the two Bothwells and called them both Claudius.

Now, it seems to me that a very similar method of construction has been followed in the case of *Macbeth*. Here also Shakespeare is mainly interested in the history of James I; as we have seen he was probably writing the play for direct presentation before the king and at a moment when James had especial cause for apprehension.

James quite seriously believed that he was the destined restorer of the Arthurian Empire, that prophecies centuries before his birth had announced the coming of a king who should unite the whole island under one crown. James quite seriously believed that, during the greater part of his life, he had been the object of special attention on the part of the powers of evil: wizards, witches and wicked spirits of all kinds whose intention was, under the immediate direction of Satan himself, to prevent the Union of the Crowns. The king further believed that his personal enemy—the younger Bothwell—had been closely associated with these witches and wizards, had been aided, abetted and urged on by them in various attempts on the king's life, and he believed this on the definite evidence of the criminal trials themselves, on the sworn testimony of many witnesses and the decisions of the most eminent judges on the Scottish Bench[1].

It is not fair to accuse James of any special superstition because he believed in witches; the ministers of his Kirk, his most eminent judges, his Privy Council themselves, agreed with him. Moreover the Privy Council had recently ascribed the terrible though frustrated attempt of Gunpowder Plot to the evil spirits of Scotland, the same presumably who had tormented James in his earlier life.

I believe that Shakespeare has blent these motives with the motives of the Darnley murder. I have already shown how the motive of prophecy, in which James firmly believed, is interwoven in the play[2], and I will now proceed to show how the motives connected with Francis, Earl Bothwell are interwoven in the play.

Francis, Earl Bothwell had an undoubted connection with witches and warlocks: Sir James Melville says in his *Memoirs*:

About this time (i.e. 1591) many witches were tane in Lowdien who deponit of some attempts made by the Earl Bothwell, as they alleged, against his Majesty's person. Whilk comming to the said Earl's ears, he entered in ward within the Castle of Edinburgh desiring to be tried; alleging that the Devil, who was a liar from the beginning, nor yet his sworn witches ought not to be credited.

[1] Pitcairn's *Ancient Scottish Criminal Trials.*   [2] Chap. I.

Specially a renowned midwife called Anny Sampsown, affirmed that she, in company with nine other witches, being convened in the night beside Prestonpans, the devil their master being present standing in the midst of them; there a body of wax shapen and made by the said Anny Sampsown, wrapped within a linen cloth, was first delivered to the devil; which, after he had pronounced his verde, delivered the said picture to Anny Sampsown, and she to her next marrow, and so everyone round about, saying this is King James the sixt, ordered to be consumed at the instance of a nobleman, Francis, Earl Bothwell.

Among the "articles of dittay" against Agnes Sampsown (Jan. 27th, 1590) which were in all fifty-three in number were the following:

(12) Convict that she foreknew of the devil and told Patrick Porteous that he would live but eleven years.

    *   *   *   *   *   *

(33) Convict that the first time...she began to serve the devil, was after the death of her husband, and that he appeared to her in likeness of a man...after that he appointed time and place for their night meeting.

    *   *   *   *   *   *

(35) Convict...for sailing with certain of her accomplices...to a ship called the "Grace of God" in which she entered...and at her being there saw not the mariners, neither saw they her; and when they came away, the devil raised an evil wind, he being under the ship, and caused the ship to perish.

    *   *   *   *   *   *

(46) Describes how with a number of others she "raised storms to stay the Queen's home-coming to Scotland."

Marion Leuchop was the person entrusted with the message: "Ye shall warn the rest of the sisters to raise the wind this day, at eleven hours, to stay the Queen's coming in Scotland."

They were to "make the storm universal through the sea."

Agnes Sampsown, it might be remarked, was executed.

---

[1] Pitcairn's *Ancient Scottish Criminal Trials.*

Now here we surely have close parallels with *Macbeth*. We have the connection between James' most dangerous enemy—Francis, Earl Bothwell—and a witch and we have Earl Bothwell practising against the king's life by means of the witch; we have the witch employing the very practices of the witches in *Macbeth*, raising storms and so forth.

With the "articles of dittay" against Agnes Sampsown we may compare the speeches in *Macbeth*[1].

> SECOND WITCH. I 'll give thee a wind.
> FIRST   ,,   Thou 'rt kind.
> THIRD   ,,   And I another.
> FIRST   ,,   I myself have all the other,
>   And the very ports they blow,
>   All the quarters that they know
>   I' the shipman's card.

Agnes Sampsown and her comrades have the power to make people waste away; so have the witches in *Macbeth*[2].

> Weary se'nnights, nine times nine
> Shall he dwindle, peak, and pine!
> Though his bark cannot be lost,
> Yet it shall be tempest-tost.

Agnes Sampsown and her comrades have the gift of prophecy just as the witches have in *Macbeth*.

Francis, Earl Bothwell was again accused of complicity in witchcraft in the course of the trial of Euphemia Mackalzane. She was a lady of very good social position. Pitcairn sums up the subject:

That a person, moving in the rank of society which Euphemia occupied, should have leagued with the obscure and profligate wretches who figure in the trials for witchcraft at this period, for the destruction of her sovereign, and that too by such unlikely and absurd means, seems irreconcilable with any ideas of sanity which can now be formed. It is evident, however,

---

[1] I. iii.   [2] I. iii.

that she believed herself as well as her associates, to be possessed of supernatural powers; and that she had the firmest reliance in infernal agency. The only reason which can be assigned for such frantic and detestable conduct seems to be, that she was devoted to the ancient Roman Catholic faith, and thus bearing personal hatred against the King and the Reformed Religion; she was besides a zealous partisan of Bothwell and proved herself capable of using every means which he might suggest, or which she herself perversely considered to be most calculated to advance his interests and the predominance of her party. It is worthy of remark that three days before Ewsame's cremation, Bothwell "broke out of the Castle of Edinburgh" who had been there, in prison, some 20 days before, for alleged witchcraft and consulting with witches, especially with one Richard Grahame, to conspire the King's death; and upon the 25th of June, the said Earl of Bothwell was forfaulted and intimation made thereof, by open proclamation at the cross of Edinburgh. It is known that Bothwell had much traffic with witches, and was himself esteemed an expert necromancer.

This passage is important because it shows Bothwell's legal connection with two more of the witches—Euphemia Mackalzane and Richard Grahame—and it shows that the Roman Catholic faith was a powerful impelling motive with some, at any rate, of these witches.

Another interesting passage is to be found in the proclamation alluded to above by Pitcairn at Edinburgh, June 25th, 1591, against:

Francis, sometime Earl Bothwell,...his highness, perceiving that he has given himself over altogether into the hands of Satan, and this his spirit has so mightily prevailed into him that he yet still insists, without fear of God, or respect to honesty and shame of the world, to continue in all kinds of filthiness, heaping treason upon treason, against God, his Majesty, and this his native country, ever assisting such persons by force, counsel and otherwise, as were and are enemies to God, his highness, and sought the subversion of the true religion, taking the maintenance of traitors, murderers and other wicked persons, who to impetrate impunity of their wicked lives and liberty to do evil at all times, made their dependence upon him; he having also now at last, for the better execution of his wicked intention and treasonable conspiracy against his Majesty's own person, had consultation with necromancers, witches and other wicked and ungodly persons, both without and within this country, for bereaving of his highness' life, confessed by some of the same kind...his Majesty now at last caused pronounce the Dome and Sentence of forfalture against him.

Here again we surely have the closest parallels to *Macbeth* and the motives we are studying in *Macbeth*. Here, as before, Roman Catholicism is given as an impelling motive both for Francis, Earl Bothwell and for the witches. Earl Bothwell has given himself over "into the hands of Satan" and "his spirit has prevailed mightily into him"; he has "consultations with necromancers, witches and other ungodly persons" and plans with them the murder of a king.

This is, surely, the essential idea of *Macbeth* which thus contains a close resemblance to Earl Bothwell's life.

Macbeth also plans with the witches the murder of a king and Macbeth does not doubt that their inspiration is from the Powers of Darkness:

> And be these juggling fiends no more believed[1].

Neither does Banquo doubt that they are directly inspired by the powers of evil[2]:

> And oftentimes, to win us to our harm,
> The instruments of darkness tell us truths.

Francis, Earl Bothwell takes upon himself the maintenance of "traitors, murderers and other wicked persons" who find impunity for their crimes through his protection, and this is exactly the situation in *Macbeth* for Macbeth has broken men for his servitors.

---

[1] v. viii.   [2] I. iii.

As we have seen, all the villains in Scotland do take Macbeth as their license to perpetrate crimes[1]:

> each new morn
> New widows howl, new orphans cry, new sorrows
> Strike heaven on the face.

We may compare also Masson's Preface to the *Register of the Privy Council of Scotland*:

> The younger Bothwell was a Catholic and continually engaged in Catholic conspiracies....
>
> It is from April 1591 that Bothwell steps forth...in that character of ringleader of new commotions and disorders in which he was to vex the souls of James and Maitland....
>
> ...On December 27th, 1591, he broke out where he was least expected,...actually within Holyrood Palace itself, battering at the doors of the King's chamber.
>
> ...Nor had the King ever manifested such a passion of personal anger against any political culprit such a desire for real and severe revenge, as now against Bothwell. This cousin of his own...appears to have been to him an object of personal dread....
>
> A sudden epidemic of diablerie seems to have broken out in and near Edinburgh during the King's absence in Denmark through the winter of 1589–90 and to have lasted through the whole of the next year and the next.
>
> No man of public mark, it appears, had been so deep in this witchcraft business as Bothwell, so intimate and incessant in consultations with the noted wizards and warlocks of the time, and especially with the warlock-in-chief Richie Grahame; and in that charge of high treason on which Bothwell had been arrested and imprisoned in April, 1591, and which had driven him into his subsequent course of wild rebellion, the main item had been his having conspired with such infernal agencies for the death of the King and for his own ambitions in the State as depending on that event....

Now here again we have an important development of the situation; we learn that Francis Earl Bothwell was the great centre of Catholic plots and conspiracies; that no other

[1] IV. iii.

man of importance in the realm had been so conspicuous in "diablerie" as Bothwell and so frequent in his consultations with wizards and witches; like Macbeth he had hoped to slay the king by his necromancy and, also like Macbeth, he had hoped to gratify his own ambitions in the State by so doing. Again we have the king's personal hatred of Earl Bothwell, the most detested of all James' personal enemies, which would, of course, give Shakespeare an additionally strong motive for representing him before James.

We have the fact that he is a relative of the king's, a cousin, and Duncan alludes to Macbeth in the same relationship:

> O valiant cousin! worthy gentleman!

In the fact that Bothwell had been in the habit of breaking inside the king's palaces, battering actually on the door of his chamber in Holyrood, we have perhaps a suggestion for the phrase in *Macbeth*[1]:

> I hope the days are near at hand
> That chambers will be safe.

Then again in the proclamation of June 25th, 1591, Francis Stuart is said to hold a title "to which he no ways succeeded by birth." James, in fact, gave him as a special grace the title of Earl of Bothwell and, as if that title had been fatal, he seemed to give with it the treachery and murderous propensities of the earlier holder of the title— the Hepburn. An exactly similar circumstance occurs in *Macbeth*; Macbeth fights against and vanquishes the rebel thane of Cawdor, he receives his title as a reward from the king and this very title serves him as a stepping-stone from which he proceeds to plan the murder of the king.

[1] v. iv.

Duncan says of Cawdor:

> go pronounce his present death,
> And with his former title greet Macbeth.

Ironically enough it is this very title—thane of Cawdor—
which makes Macbeth feel he can fulfil the further part of
the witch's prophecy and obtain the throne. Many critics
have commented on the tragic irony of this traitor's title
being given to Macbeth who promptly turns traitor also;
so a consultation of the *Scottish State Papers* shows how
continually the men of that age dwelt on the fact that it
was James himself who had given Francis Stuart this
unlucky title—a title which seemed destined to be fatal to
the royal house of Scotland.

In a footnote on the affairs of 1591 Masson says:

> He (i.e. Bothwell) had already, in fact, mixed himself up a
> good deal with public affairs, become one of the most powerful
> men in the kingdom, and obtained a peculiar reputation for
> political waywardness and recklessness, and for dissipation and
> profligacy....Agnes Sampsown and Richard Graham had testi-
> fied that he had consulted them as to the probable duration of
> the King's life, and what should happen to him after his death.

Once more we have parallels with *Macbeth*, for the Macbeth
of the later part of the drama is a singularly wayward and
reckless person who passes from one rashness to another.

Even the witches allude to Macbeth as "wayward[1]."

> And, which is worse, all you have done
> Hath been but for a wayward son,
> Spiteful and wrathful.

Similarly Macbeth is profligate and given to every form
of dissipation[2]:

> I grant him bloody,
> Luxurious, avaricious, false, deceitful,
> Sudden, malicious, smacking of every sin
> That has a name.

[1] III. v.   [2] IV. iii.

This description, as I have pointed out before, would apply also to the elder Bothwell; but then it was precisely the likeness between them which awakened the superstitious horror of the age. Macbeth, we may observe, was practically a madman in his later stages, and this appears to have been true also of Bothwell.

Masson in his *Introduction to the Register of the Privy Council of Scotland* speaks of

the weary business of the inextinguishable Bothwell. For fifteen months already this half-mad cousin of the King's, with no definable policy but the mere incarnation of general dis-content, had been a thorn in his Majesty's side...though chased again and again condemned and forfalted, he was still at large....

Once again there is the plain suggestion of motives for Macbeth; in the later stages of the play Macbeth becomes so frenzied that he does indeed seem half-mad.

CHAPTER VI

THE WITCHES IN *MACBETH* AND THE SCOTTISH WITCH-TRIALS

WE may observe that Shakespeare took but little of the material of his witch-scenes from Holinshed. All that Holinshed gives is the witches' prophecy to Macbeth and Banquo.

He says that the two generals were passing through "woods and fields" when in a "laund" (i.e. an open space) three women met them "in strange and wild apparel, resembling creatures of an elder world"; they give their prophecies to Macbeth and Banquo and then disappear.

"Afterwards," says Holinshed, "The common opinion was, that these women were either the weird sisters, that is (as ye would say) the goddesses of destinie, or else some nymphs or feiries, indued with knowledge of prophesie by their necro-manticall science, bicause everie thing came to pass as they had spoken."

Now this is absolutely all Holinshed has to say on the matter; he gives no further details.

All the wonderful and terrible details of the witch-scenes are added by Shakespeare himself, and I shall have no difficulty in showing that they correspond in the closest possible manner with the actual details of the Scottish witch-trials, especially those connected with Francis, Earl Bothwell. Not one of these details seems to be invented, on the contrary they are studied with an almost meticulous accuracy; but Shakespeare, here as elsewhere, is a master of selection and reveals his genius in an unrivalled power of tragic concentration and compression.

It is notable that Bothwell's witches had familiar spirits.

"Some of them," says Melville[1], "show how that there was a westland man, called Riche Grame, who had a familiar spirit; the whilk Riche they said, could both do and tell many things chiefly against the Earl Bothwell. Whereupon the said Richard Graham was apprehended and brought to Edinburgh; who, being examined before His Majesty, granted that he had a familiar spirit that showed him sundry things."

So also the witches possess familiar spirits[2].

One says: "I come, Graymalkin!" and the other answers "Paddock calls," Graymalkin and Paddock being apparently the names of the familiars.

Macbeth's witches also have dealings with "Hecate," the "close contriver of all harms" who comes direct from "the pit of Acheron[3]."

When they are brewing their hell-broth another spirit—Harpier—attends them[4].

Harpier cries, "'Tis time, 'tis time," and when Macbeth visits them, they ask him if he wishes to hear their prophecies from their own mouths or the mouths of their masters and he answers: "Call 'em; let me see 'em," upon which they summon the spirits.

The witches in the Scottish criminal trials were accused of the gift of prophecy. Agnes or Anny Sampsown (tried January 27th, 1590) was, as we have seen, one of those most closely connected with Francis Stuart. Among the accusations brought against her was this gift of prophecy. Thus the Articles of Dittay include:

(13) That she was made foreknown of the devil, of the last Michaelmas storm, and that there would be great scathe, both by sea and land.

(14) Item, that she was made foreknown by the spirit that the Queen's Majesty would never come in this country unless the king fetched her.

---

[1] *Memoirs.*   [2] I. i.   [3] III. v.   [4] IV. i.

Now this is, of course, exactly the mechanism employed in *Macbeth*. The weird sisters throughout have the gift of prophecy; they know the issue of the battle and they know that Macbeth and Banquo are approaching before Macbeth and Banquo appear. They win Macbeth's confidence by prophesying to him that he will be thane of Cawdor, and so obtain a hold on him which incites him to his crime. Moreover it is quite obvious from the last of the witch-scenes[1] that it is their attendant spirits and not they themselves who possess the gift of prophecy, since in the passage already quoted they ask Macbeth if he will hear the future from them or from their masters.

Agnes Sampsown as we have seen and the other Scottish witches were accused of raising storms and pursuing ships while themselves invisible. It was believed especially that the coming of Anne of Denmark had been delayed through these witch-raised storms.

Article 46 describes how Agnes with a number of others "raised storms to stay the Queen's home-coming to Scotland."

The same accusations were brought against Euphemia Mackalzane[2].

(25) Item. Indited and accused for a convention held by you and other notorious witches...where you and they took the sea, Robert Grierson being your admiral and master-man, past over the sea in riddles to a ship; where you entered with the devil your master therein; when, after you had eaten and drunken you cast over a black dog that skipped under the ship, and thereby, ye having the Devil your master therein, who drowned the ship...whereby the Queen was put back by storm.

[1] IV. i.
[2] Pitcairn's *Ancient Scottish Criminal Trials*.

Pitcairn in his *A True Discourse of the Apprehension of Sundry Witches lately taken in Scotland* (i.e. in 1591) writes:

> Againe it is confessed that the said christened cat was the cause that the King's Majesty's ship, at his coming forth of Denmark had a contrary wind to the rest of the ships then being in his company; which thing was most true and strange, as the King's Majesty acknowledged, for when the rest of the ships had a fair and good wind, then was the wind contrary and altogether against his Majesty; and further, the said witch declared that his Majesty had never come safely from the sea, if his faith had not prevailed above their intentions.

Here we obviously have again the closest parallels with the witches in *Macbeth*.

They are from the beginning associated with storms[1]:

> When shall we three meet again,
> In thunder, lightning or in rain?

In a later scene[2] a witch tells how a sailor's wife has insulted her and how, like Euphemia, the witch means to sail after the husband in a sieve and, in the guise of an animal, "like a rat without a tail," destroy him. In exactly the same way the Scottish witches sailed in sieves and either they or their spirits disguised themselves as animals, and so destroyed the ships.

There is a perfectly similar incident to the vain attempt to destroy the king in the lines:

> Though his bark cannot be lost,
> Yet it shall be tempest-tost.

The Scottish witches term themselves "sisters"; so, of course, do Macbeth's:

> Sister, where thou[3]?
> Betimes I will to the weird sisters[4].

---

[1] I. i.   [2] I. iii.
[3] I. iii.   [4] III. iv.

The Scottish witches can pass over the sea as well as the land; so can those of *Macbeth* for they call themselves

> Posters of the sea and land[1].

Again Macbeth speaks of the terrific storms they raise[2]:

> Though you untie the winds, and let them fight
> Against the churches; though the yesty waves
> Confound and swallow navigation up;
> Though bladed corn be lodg'd, and trees blown down;
> Though castles topple on their warders' heads.

The association of cats with witchcraft has, of course, often been observed. They are mentioned in the extracts quoted above and repeatedly in *Macbeth*. Thus, in the first scene, there is a reference to "Graymalkin," a name for a cat and meaning, presumably, a spirit disguised as a cat; before the entrance of Macbeth the cat-spirit gives a signal[3]:

> Thrice the brinded cat hath mew'd.

The ingredients used in the hell-broth in *Macbeth* have also their close parallels in the Scottish witch-trials.

Thus in the trial of Patrick Loucy[4] (July 23rd, 1605) he was accused:

> Of consorting with one Janet Hunter, a notorious witch, and who was executed to the death for sorcery and witchcraft... which Janet and the said Patrick...convened themselves upon the common waste sandhills in Kyle...where the Devil appeared to them and conferred with them...there appeared to them a devilish spirit in likeness to a woman and calling herself Helen M'bune.
>
> ...At diverse times thereafter they assembled themselves in diverse kirks and kirkyards; where the said Patrick and his associates aforesaid, raised and took up sundry dead persons out of their graves, and dismembered the said dead corpses for the practising of their witchcraft and sorcery.

[1] i. iii.   [2] iv. i.
[3] iv. i.   [4] Pitcairn.

This trial is interesting as it had occurred only such a short time before the actual date of *Macbeth*. We see here the gathering of the witches on a waste place, the sandhills; in *Macbeth* also they appear in a "desert place[1]" and their next meeting is to be with Macbeth on a heath. A devilish spirit appears to them in the likeness of a woman, just as Hecate appears in *Macbeth*[2], and they dismember corpses for the purpose of their sorcery. The witches in *Macbeth* certainly do this. In the scene concerning the sailor and the storms[3] we have the boast of the first witch:

> Here I have a pilot's thumb,
> Wreck'd as homeward he did come,

and in the witch-broth[4] they boil:

> Liver of blaspheming Jew;...
> Nose of Turk and Tartar's lips;
> Finger of birth-strangled babe,
> Ditch-delivered by a drab.

There does not seem much room for doubt that Bothwell and Richard Grahame had really tried to poison the king by means of such a hell-broth.

Thus we have a trial in 1591 for a "Wilful Error in Assise—that of Acquitting a Witch[5]":

Barbara Napier was accused of seeking help from Richard Graham, a notorious sorcerer...and specially...for fear the Earl Bothwell should have entered in Edinburgh, she declared to the said Richard, that she heard a woman say, that our sovereign lord would get scathe by a toad or gangrell...who consulted with the spirit thereanent and received by his response, that his Majesty would be troubled by convention of women, through the dropping of a toad...there were assembled nine principals....Agnes Sampsown proposed the de-

---

[1] I. i.   [2] III. v.   [3] I. iii.
[4] IV. i.   [5] Pitcairn.

struction of his highness' person, saying to the Devil: "We have a turn ado, and we would fain be at it if we could and therefore help us to it....The Devil answered he would do what he could, but it would be long to, because it would be thwarted, and...he ordered them to hang, roast and drop a toad and to lay the drops of the toad mixed with strong wash (i.e. stale urine) an adder skin, and the thing in the forehead of a new foaled foal in his Highness' way...wherever it might drop upon his Highness' head or body, for his Highness' destruction, that another might have ruled in his Majesty's place....Margaret Thomsown was appointed to drop the toad.

And the said Barbara was accused that she gave her bodily presence upon Allhallow evening last (1590) to the convention held at the Kirk, North-Berwick, where she danced along the kirkyard....Agnes Sampsown and her daughter and all the rest following the said Barbara....At the which place and time the women first paid homage, and were turned six times widdershins about....

There were three dead bodies taken up and jointed; the nails and joints were parted amongst them; the Devil commanded them to keep the joints upon them while the same dried and then to make a powder of them to do evil with.

There are several points of comparison here. These witches also, we observe, belong to the Bothwell gang of diablerie. We observe also the peculiar prominence given to toads in their sorcery. This, of course, is equally true of *Macbeth*. In the opening scene[1] one of the spirits appears as "Paddock" (i.e. a toad), and it is the first ingredient to be thrown into the hell-broth[2]:

> Round about the cauldron go;
> In the poison'd entrails throw.
> Toad, that under cold stone
> Days and nights hast thirty-one
> Swelter'd venom sleeping got,
> Boil thou first i' the charmèd pot.

Another ingredient used in this Bothwell witch-trial is

[1] I. i.   [2] IV. i.

an adder skin and it is the second ingredient in the *Macbeth* hell-broth:

> Fillet of a fenny snake
> In the cauldron boil and bake;

and in addition there is the

> Adder's fork, and blind-worm's sting,

and

> Eye of newt, and toe of frog.

The dancing is another important element in the Bothwell witch-trial and in *Macbeth's* witches. Bothwell's witches dance in multiples of three: "nine principals" and the number of their dances is in multiples of three "six times" and they also dance in contrary directions, "widdershins" or contrary to the course of the sun; the number of dead bodies jointed is "three."

So in *Macbeth* we have the weird sisters dancing whenever they wish their charms to be particularly strong; they dance when they meet Macbeth first and their dances are multiples of three:

> Thus do go about, about;
> Thrice to thine and thrice to mine
> And thrice again, to make up nine.
> Peace! the charm's wound up.

So also they dance when brewing the hell-broth[1]:

> Round about the cauldron go,

and, when Hecate enters to meet the three witches, she says:

> And now about the cauldron sing,
> Like elves and fairies in a ring,
> Enchanting all that you put in.

Bothwell's witches held their assemblies mainly at night and Macbeth addresses his as

> You secret, black and midnight hags.

[1] IV. i.

It is important to remember that James himself had examined some of these witches and taken part in their trials.

Pitcairn in the work already referred to, *A True Discourse of the Apprehension of Sundry Witches lately taken in Scotland* (1591), has the following references to the king's direct participation:

> ...The King himself examined Agnes Sampsown...she confessed that upon the night of Allhallow E'en last, she was accompanied, as well with the persons aforesaide, as also with a great many other witches, to the number of two hundred, and that all together went to Sea, each one in a riddle or cive, and went into the same with flagons of wine, making merry and drinking by the way, in the same riddles or cives to the Kirk of North-Berwick in Lothian, and that, after they had landed, took hands on the land, and danced this reel or short dance, singing all with one voice....Geillis Duncane went before them, playing this reel or dance, upon a small trumpe, called a Jew's trump, until they entered into the kirk of North-Berwick.
> ...These confessions made the King in a wonderful admiration, and sent for the said Geillis Duncane, who upon the like trump did play the said dance before the King's Majesty.

Here again we see the close relation to the motives of Macbeth; we have the sailing in sieves, the dancing and singing and we see that James himself was personally and deeply interested.

In the same work we read:

> The Devil himself met them and did greatly inveigh against the King of Scotland, he received their oaths for their good and true service towards him and departed....At which time, the witches demanded of the Devil, "Why he did bear such hatred to the King," who answered: "By reason the King is the greatest enemy he had in the world."

Various people seem to have objected to James' presence

at these witch-trials on the ground that it was very dangerous both for himself and his realm; but the writer argues:

It is well known that the King is the child and servant of God, and they but the servants of the Devil; he is the Lord's anointed and they but the vessels of God's wrath; he is a true Christian and trusteth in God; they worse than infidels for they only trust in the Devil, who daily serves them till he have brought them to utter destruction.

We have here exactly the same idea as in *Macbeth* that the service of the powers of darkness is meant to lead men on to their doom. Banquo warns Macbeth:

> oftentimes, to win us to our harm,
> The instruments of darkness tell us truths,
> Win us with honest trifles, to betray 's
> In deepest consequence[1],

and Macbeth himself knows it before the end[2]:

> I pull in resolution, and begin
> To doubt the equivocation of the fiend
> That lies like truth.

We are now in a position to see exactly what the *Macbeth* witch-scenes meant for James the First.

(1) James believed that he had all his life been persecuted by the powers of evil, directly inspired by the Devil, who were determined to prevent his accession to the throne of England, because by this accession he would become the monarch of a United Great Britain and the head of a great Protestant empire.

(2) These witches and powers of evil had been in league with the king's most hated personal enemy—Francis, Earl Bothwell—had helped him by prophesying future events and had egged him on to attempt the murder of the king.

(3) Francis, Earl Bothwell, was more deeply involved in

---

[1] I. iii.   [2] V. v.

the practices of witchcraft than any other man of rank in Scotland.

(4) The Scottish witches associated, so it was believed, with evil spirits which appeared in the form of animals. Macbeth's witches also associate with evil spirits which appear in the form of cats and toads.

(5) The Scottish witches associated with a devilish spirit in the form of a woman. So do Macbeth's witches associate with a devilish spirit in the form of a woman—Hecate.

(6) The Scottish witches sailed on the sea in sieves. So do Macbeth's witches sail on the sea in sieves.

(7) The Scottish witches had power to raise storms and tempests and attempted, though unsuccessfully, to destroy the king by this means.

So also do Macbeth's witches raise storms and tempests.

(8) The Scottish witches had the power of distressing vessels and sometimes sinking them.

Macbeth's witches also have the power of distressing vessels and sometimes sinking them.

(9) The Scottish witches made use of ceremonial dances, contrary to the course of the sun, "widdershins." Three and multiples of three were their sacred numbers. So also do Macbeth's witches make use of ceremonial dances; three and multiples of three are their sacred numbers.

(10) The Scottish witches dismembered dead bodies and used the portions in charms. So also do Macbeth's witches dismember dead bodies and use the portions in charms.

(11) The Scottish witches employed toads and adders for purposes of sorcery.

Macbeth's witches use toads and adders for purposes of sorcery.

(12) The Scottish witches possessed the power of prophecy. Macbeth's witches possess the power of prophecy.

(13) The prophetic gift of the Scottish witches was really due to their familiars.

The prophetic power of Macbeth's witches is really due not to themselves but to their familiars.

(14) The Scottish witches were in the habit of telling men half-truths and so obtaining influence over them.

Macbeth's witches also tell him half-truths and so lead him on to his ruin.

(15) The Scottish witches egged Bothwell on to murder the king by prophesying the king's death.

So do Macbeth's witches egg him on to murder Duncan by prophesying his own accession.

(16) The Scottish witches loved waste and desolate places like sandhills and heaths and were fond of meeting by night. So also do Macbeth's witches love waste and desolate places and so also are they fond of meeting by night.

It seems to me that it would be hardly possible for Shakespeare to have concentrated more resemblances or closer resemblances in the brief space at his disposal. When we remember that these witch-trials were of special interest to James I, that Shakespeare was writing just after Gunpowder Plot and that the Privy Council of Scotland themselves had told James that the plot was "excogitated" by evil spirits, we may feel sure that here also Shakespeare was making use of historic material.

The main aim of the Bothwell witches who were set on or supposed to be set on by the Roman Catholics was to prevent the Union of England and Scotland, and Gunpowder Plot also had been aimed at that Union.

The demonstration seems to be complete.

Note. It is worthy of note that Catherine de Médici was accused by the Huguenots of very similar witch-practices. An account of them even more horrible than the account I have given above will be found in D'Aubigné's *Les Tragiques.*

See also Appendix A.   8—2

CHAPTER VII

MACBETH AND THE MASSACRE OF
ST BARTHOLOMEW

I HAVE shown that, at the time *Macbeth* was written, the Massacre of St Bartholomew was much in the minds of the people of England because the Gunpowder Plot seemed to them to resemble that massacre and possibly to be a precursor to one very similar.

Now it seems to me that Shakespeare also has this parallel in mind and has applied it more than once in *Macbeth*.

Compare, for one thing, the way in which the unhappy Charles IX wavered and was urged on by his mother with the taunt of cowardice. De Thou narrates

The Queen went at midnight to the chamber of the king, fearing that he would change his resolution, because he seemed to her to waver and the atrocity of the action put him in doubt. The Queen, seeing that the king still hesitated, blamed him fiercely for losing by delay this magnificent opportunity of exterminating his enemies which God had given him. This Prince (Charles) who was very proud and accustomed to shed blood, feeling himself accused of cowardice, was angry at her discourse and commanded that the thing should be done.

Now here we surely have very close parallels to *Macbeth*; the woman urges the man to something which he has previously promised. No such interview and previous promise is recorded in the actual text of *Macbeth*, and its absence has been one of the standing problems of commentators who, in consequence, have assumed an interview not recorded in the play.

In the next place we have the woman dwelling on the magnificent opportunity:

> Nor time, nor place,
> Did then adhere, and yet you would make both.
> They have made themselves, and that their fitness now
> Does unmake you[1].

There is the wavering and withdrawal of Macbeth and his plea for his victim:

> He hath honoured me of late: and I have bought
> Golden opinions from all sorts of people,

and there is the woman's taunt of cowardice: "live a coward in thine own esteem," and the man's anger at the taunt:

> I dare do all that may become a man.

Now all these circumstances show a close parallel to the history of St Bartholomew and not one of them occurs in the literary source—Holinshed.

Holinshed says nothing of a previous promise given by the man, he says nothing of the man's wavering and hesitating; he does say that Macbeth's wife urged her husband on; but he does not say that she used the taunt of cowardice, reminded him of his previous promise, and dwelt on the unrivalled excellence of the opportunity.

De Thou says:

> The queen took advantage of his anger, and, still fearing that he would relent, gave a signal for the bell of St Germain L'Auxerrois to be sounded.

So is the bell, we remember, the signal for the hesitating Macbeth who hears it with terror and with fear.

The dreadful Catherine urged her son on to dissimulate. De Thou tells us that she informed Charles that the man who could not dissimulate was unworthy to be a king; her

---

[1] I. vii.

son's soubriquet for her was "Madame la serpente." So in
Lady Macbeth we have the passion for dissimulation[1]:

> To beguile the time,
> Look like the time; bear welcome in your eye,
> Your hand, your tongue: look like the innocent flower
> But be the serpent under 't.

Then there is the hesitation of Lady Macbeth before the
immediate presence of the deed and her curious statement
that she would have killed Duncan herself had he not re-
sembled her father; there is certainly no suggestion of this
in Holinshed who says nothing of any hesitation and nothing
of any likeness to a father.

But there was a suggestion in the history of St Bartholomew; Catherine de Médici had been accustomed to address
Coligny as "father" and she certainly did hesitate before
his murder; she had decided to countermand the order, but
was told it was too late.

Jean de Serres says:

> To the guilty plotters that was a sleepless night. Unable to
> rest quietly, at a little before dawn, Catherine with her two
> elder sons found her way to the portal of the Louvre....They
> heard a pistol-shot....Hastily they sent a servant to the Duke
> of Guise and countermanded the instructions of the evening
> and bade him do no injury to the admiral. It was too late....
> The mother and her sons returned hastily to their former
> purpose.

The striking on the bell plays a prominent part in *Macbeth*
and everyone remembers the terrible incident in the massacre
of St Bartholomew of the signal given by the sounding of
the tocsin of St Germain L'Auxerrois.

It was Catherine herself, as we have seen, who gave the
order for the sounding of the bell, and in *Macbeth* it is Lady

[1] I. v.

Macbeth who herself strikes the bell and herself gives the signal.

Catherine was very impatient, fearing lest Charles, considering the Heinousness of such deeds, should alter his mind... she was willing to begin without any further delay...she ordered the ringing of the bell of St Germain L'Auxerrois[1].

There can be no doubt of the terrible effectiveness on the stage of this incident—the striking on the bell—and, if the incident is so impressive to us, it would have been far more impressive to that audience at that time. One must remember that Shakespeare would be likely to choose for representation on the stage not only those events which were dramatic and terrible in themselves; but that, as a popular dramatist, he would also have the strongest possible reasons for employing just those events which would affect his audience most.

Motives like the witches, like the dagger, like the striking on the bell, were already symbols of horror. Why not use the symbols of horror?

Another terribly effective detail is that of the attendants who are praying when the murderer—Macbeth—comes upon them. This also may have been suggested by Coligny's murder, for de Thou tells us that Coligny and his people were at prayers when the assassins reached the door. So we have Macbeth[2]:

> I stood and heard them:
> But they did say their prayers, and address'd them
> Again to sleep...
> One cried "God bless us!" and "Amen" the other:
> As they had seen me with these hangman's hands.
> Listening their fear, I could not say "Amen,"
> When they did say "God bless us!"

[1] Laval, *History of the Reformation in France.*
[2] II. ii.

There is, of course, no such incident in Holinshed. There are, it seems to me, further parallels in the murder of Banquo.

In Holinshed the occasion for the murder of Banquo is a supper:

> He willed therefore the same Banquho with his son named Fleance, to come to a supper that he had prepared for them, which was indeed, as he had devised, present death at the hands of certain murderers, whom he hired to execute that deed, appointing them to meet with the same Banquho and his sonne without the palace, as they returned to their lodgings, and there to slay them, so that he would not have his house slandered, but that in time to come he might clear himself.

Now here again, as in the case of the Darnley murder, there is a natural parallel between the source and the historical event; and here also, as in the case of the Darnley murder, Shakespeare has intensified that parallel by the details he has added.

I need hardly remind the reader that the occasion for the massacre of St Bartholomew was the marriage-feast of Henry of Navarre with Marguerite of Valois and that the hideous treachery of making an invitation to a festival the occasion of a massacre was the common theme of all the Huguenot historians of France. No circumstance was dwelt upon with more anger and more horror by the Protestant world.

We may compare what Nat Lee says in *The Massacre of Paris*:

> A reconcilement, with a wedding Feast,
> While murder was the Treat of ev'ry Guest.

So in *Macbeth* everything is done to intensify the horror of this initial situation. Macbeth dwells, as strongly as possible, on the great honour he is paying to Banquo; Banquo was to have been the principal guest; everything was to have been done to honour him and all the time Banquo's destiny was the most grisly of murders at the hands of his royal host. This is an almost exact parallel to the fate of Coligny who also was to have been the most honoured guest at a royal festival, who also was flattered to the full by his royal host and hostess and who also was murdered with the most grisly of murders.

Coligny, when the murderers came upon him, besought his people with quiet dignity to escape and most of them did so, he himself facing the murderers with undismayed courage. So Banquo at once cries out to Fleance to flee. Here again the parallel to the history is far closer than it is to the source for Holinshed only says that, owing to the darkness of the night, Fleance escaped. He does not say that, with quiet dignity, Banquo had told him to go.

Another parallel lies in the use of torches. The massacre of St Bartholomew was largely conducted by torch-light in the streets of Paris, and the murderers of Coligny carried torches. Jean de Serres states that torches were burning all night in the streets to make the task of the assassins easy. The murdered Huguenots saw a number of torches and then armed men approaching.

So it is with the murder of Banquo. By the light of torches Banquo was slain[1]. Now of this detail again Holinshed says nothing. Here also, just as in the striking of the bell, Shakespeare had an incident dramatic and dreadful in itself and also one that especially appealed to the nerves of his audience.

Neither does Holinshed give any details as to the actual murder of Banquo. He only says that he was slain.

The murder of Coligny was, in all its details, particularly horrible; he was struck repeatedly upon the head, covered with blood and terribly disfigured. This is exactly what happens in the case of Banquo whose hideous dis-

[1] III. iii.

figurement so haunts Macbeth. I will place the passages side by side. De Thou says,

> Besme gave him (i.e. Coligny) a blow of the sword in his body and then another in the mouth which disfigured his face very greatly. He was not satisfied with that but heaped upon him blow after blow. Coligny's corpse, all disfigured with blood, was thrown through the window and, so great was his mutilation, that Guise who was waiting to see the last of his enemy, could not even recognise him until he had wiped the blood from his face with his handkerchief. The body was dragged through the gutters of the streets and thrown into the Seine.

De Thou further tells us that, after the body had been dragged about in "les ruisseaux de la ville de Paris," by a band of inhuman boys, the head was carried to the Louvre where Catherine and Charles feasted their eyes upon the spectacle.

We may compare *Macbeth*[1] and the way in which the whole scene is made to reek with Banquo's blood and with the ignominies offered to his dead body:

MAC. There 's blood upon thy face.
MUR. 'Tis Banquo's then.
*   *   *   *   *

MAC.   But Banquo 's safe?
MUR. Ay, my good lord: safe in a ditch he bides,
    With twenty trenchèd gashes on his head;
    The least a death to nature.

Banquo, then, was murdered like Coligny with repeated blows upon the head and a terrible amount of blood, and it is exactly in that guise that he haunts Macbeth:

MAC. Thou canst not say I did it: never shake
    Thy gory locks at me.
*   *   *   the time has been,
    That, when the brains were out, the man would die,
    And there an end; but now, they rise again,
    With twenty mortal murders on their crowns,
    And push us from our stools.

[1] III. iv.

We may also observe that just as Coligny's body was dragged along gutters and thrown into the Seine so a similar ignominy was offered to Banquo's body which was flung into a ditch.

No such details are given by Holinshed.

We may also compare the curious and dreadful interest Charles IX took in the faces of the dying: de Thou tells us that he went to look upon Briquemaut and Cavagnes when they were executed: "and caused candles to be put all over the Gibbet that he might see what mouths and faces they made in dying."

Ever afterwards he was haunted by the faces of his victims.

So in *Macbeth*:

> Avaunt! and quit my sight! Let the earth hide thee!...
> Thou hast no speculation in those eyes
> Which thou dost glare with!

After the massacre of St Bartholomew Charles IX suffered from a really terrible remorse.

De Thou tells us that Charles, who at no time slept well, used to have his night's rest broken by the memory of the dreadful scenes of the massacre, so that he seemed to die largely of remorse. The Huguenots regarded it as strange, if not miraculous, that the king who had deluged his realm in blood should perish of a malady which caused blood to exude from every pore of his body.

It was certainly singular enough to excite the attention of the world.

Charles IX, we are told, continually cried out to those around him, even while he was in his sleep, his horror of blood.

Laval says of Charles IX:

He suffered the most exquisite pains and was seen almost swimming in his own blood which came out of the body through all the usual passages and through the pores; but who could express the remorse and tortures of his soul: "Ah, Nurse," he said, the day before his death. "How much blood! How many murders!.... O my God forgive me, and vouchsafe to be merciful to me."

Macbeth also suffers from terrible dreams[1]: he speaks of:

the affliction of these terrible dreams,
That shake us nightly; better be with the dead,
Whom we, to gain our peace, have sent to peace,
* * * Duncan is in his grave;
After life's fitful fever, he sleeps well.

So we have Lady Macbeth in her sleep, like Charles IX, crying out with horror at the blood and finding it exuding from the pores of her hands:

"Here's the smell of the blood still: all the perfumes of Arabia will not sweeten this little hand."

"How she rubs her hands. It is an accustomed action with her to seem thus washing her hands; I have known her to continue in this a quarter-of-an-hour[2]."

De Thou narrates how the corpses of the Huguenots were dragged along in the mud and the number of the murders was so great that the blood filled the gutters and flowed into the rivers, staining them crimson.

Such a circumstance naturally struck horror to the hearts of the Protestants and, in the Huguenot Memoirs already alluded to, many of the Huguenot poets refer to it[3]:

Atro fluentem sanguine Sequanum
Expavit horrens Oceanus pater.
* * * * *
Garumna caesos et Liger haud potes
Referre * * *
At vos scelesti, perfida pectora,
Stricto profusis ense cruoribus,
Terras et undas aerémque
Tingite, mulciberisque flammas.
* * * * *
Vindex, Olympo scilicet arbiter
Mortalium es.

---

[1] III. ii.   [2] v. i.   [3] Published by Heinrich Wolf, 1576.

This idea of the Seine, the Loire and the Garonne bearing the blood down to the ocean, of Father Ocean himself shuddering with horror at the blood and of this blood staining alike the waves and the earth, that and the impossibility of the criminals escaping justice surely reminds us of the great lines in *Macbeth*:

> Will all great Neptune's ocean wash this blood
> Clean from my hand? No; this my hand will rather
> The multitudinous seas incarnadine,
> Making the green one red[1].

This idea does not occur in one poem only, but repeatedly, and it is easy to see how it might have kindled the terrible imagination of Shakespeare.

We must remember that Shakespeare would have had at least three important reasons for using such circumstances in his poetry: (*a*) they were intensely dramatic in themselves, (*b*) because of their associations they appealed particularly to the nerves of his audience, (*c*) the men of his time regarded them with religious horror.

D'Aubigné quotes Henry IV as his authority for saying that Charles IX after the massacre was troubled with all kinds of hallucinations; he was often distressed by visions and heard voices in the air:

he (i.e. Henry IV) had been an eye-witness of the fact and he never related it without shuddering. The Massacre was a lasting torment to the king to his very last breath...his looks and countenance were quite altered, and he grew much more sour than before, his mother and bloody councillors became to him objects of the utmost hatred; what added to his sorrow was that he saw himself deceived in his expectation for he had been made to believe that the destruction of the Admiral... would be the end of all divisions...the Medals struck represented him as having conquered the Hydra...but a hundred heads sprang from the one he had severed.

[1] II. ii.

Now here again we surely have remarkable parallels to Macbeth.

There are the hallucinations and the voices in the air. So do hallucinations play a prominent part in the mental history of Macbeth, the hallucination of the dagger floating before him, now unstained and now stained with blood, the hallucination of Banquo's ghost which nobody else sees but which to his eyes appears, disappears and re-appears.

There is also the terrible voice in the air which cries after the murder of Duncan:

> "Sleep no more!
> Macbeth does murder sleep,"...
> Still it cried "Sleep no more!" to all the house:
> "Glamis hath murder'd sleep, and therefore Cawdor
> Shall sleep no more; Macbeth shall sleep no more![1]"

It will be observed that the voice in the air pronounced exactly the same doom of sleeplessness which did come upon the unhappy Charles IX. It was largely through want of sleep that Charles died; the doom threatened to Macbeth was Charles' doom.

Now all these circumstances are added by Shakespeare; there is not the slightest foundation for them in Holinshed. Holinshed has nothing to say either of the hallucination of the dagger or of the hallucination of Banquo's ghost or of the voices in the air or of the cause which deprived Macbeth of sleep. All these things are to be found in the history of St Bartholomew. The Macbeth of Holinshed has no blood-spots upon his hand, sees no visions of a blood-stained sea, does not suffer from dreams or sleeplessness or voices or visions.

Does it not look as if Shakespeare had copied the terrible remorse of his Macbeth from that of Charles IX? Why

[1] II. ii.

should he not? His generation inherited the traditions of the religious drama; his generation believed that God still executed His moral judgments in the world, and they believed that these things were His moral judgments.

Very similar also is the solitude of Macbeth and the way he avoids even his wife:

> How now, my lord! why do you keep alone,
> Of sorriest fancies your companions making,
> Using those thoughts, which should indeed have died
> With them they think on? Things without all remedy
> Should be without regard: what's done, is done[1].

And Macbeth's reply curiously suggests the image of the hydra quoted above, the hydra the king had injured but could not slay:

> We have scotch'd the snake, not kill'd it;
> She'll close, and be herself, whilst our poor malice
> Remains in danger of her former tooth.

Another curious detail may be quoted concerning the remorse of Charles. We have D'Aubigné's authority for this:

Eight days after the massacre there came a great army of crows, some croaking and others perching on the great pavilion of the Louvre. The noise they made drew everybody to see what was the matter and the ladies were frightened and expressed their alarms to the king. That same night two hours after he was in bed, starting from his sleep, the king leaped out of bed, caused all the gentlemen to do the same and sent for Henry of Navarre, complaining that he heard a dreadful noise in the air, as it were of many voices crying, and sighing and wailing and howling; and amongst them some furiously threatening and blaspheming....The king sent his guards to stop the slaughter...they found all quiet in the city, only the skies in terrible agitation whereupon the king was more troubled than before.

[1] III. ii.

Now here again in the curious incident of the birds we surely have a likeness. There is the ominous raven who croaks at the entrance of Duncan:

> The raven himself is hoarse
> That croaks the fatal entrance of Duncan
> Under my battlements[1].

Also Macbeth is convinced that birds betray secrets and has a curious horror and fear lest they should betray his:

> It will have blood; they say, blood will have blood:
>   *   *   *   *   *   *   *
> Augurs, and understood relations, have
> By magot-pies, and choughs, and rooks brought forth
> The secret'st man of blood[2].

So also the lamentations in the air have their parallel in *Macbeth*:

> The night has been unruly: where we lay,
> Our chimneys were blown down; and, as they say,
> Lamentings heard i' the air; strange screams of death;
> And prophesying, with accents terrible,
> Of dire combustion and confus'd events,
> New hatch'd to the woeful time: the obscure bird
> Clamour'd the livelong night[3].

We have here a very close resemblance to D'Aubigné's narrative of the birds of ill-omen and the voices heard in the air, and there is no parallel passage in Holinshed.

In the Huguenot *Memoirs* I have already quoted[4], there is an epitaph on Coligny signed T.F.R. and called "Corvi ad Pseudogallos"; it runs:

> Hic ubi Parrisiis Falconia furca minatur
> Excidium, insontis pondere pressa viri,
> Supplicium rauco crocitamus gutture corvi,
> Parcentes rostro cor ferire senis,
> Exanimi senis.

---

[1] I. v.   [2] III. iv.   [3] II. iii.
[4] *Memoires de l'estat de France sous Charles IX.*

and the poem proceeds to show how the Parisians themselves are blacker and less admirable than these crows who know the truth and are reverential to the body of the dead hero.

De Thou and other contemporary historians tell us that France was deluged with vice and crime in the reign of Charles IX; the whole land was rife with lewdness, luxury, irreligion, impiety and magic abominations; besides these disorders, treason, poisoning and assassinations became so common that it was looked upon almost as a joke to destroy by these means. We may compare this with the reign of Macbeth:

> Alas, poor country!
> Almost afraid to know itself! It cannot
> Be call'd our mother, but our grave: where nothing,
> But who knows nothing, is once seen to smile;
> Where sighs, and groans, and shrieks that rend the air,
> Are made, not mark'd; where violent sorrow seems
> A modern ecstasy: the dead man's knell
> Is there scarce ask'd for who; and good men's lives
> Expire before the flowers in their caps,
> Dying or ere they sicken[1].

It is a terrible picture of a country where murderers reign, where law has disappeared and violence is rampant, and do not let us forget that it was probably what Shakespeare feared for his own country.

There is also a strange parallel in French history to the prophetic figures Macbeth sees in the magic glass. Thus in his *Deplorable Death of Henry IV*, P. Mathieu tells us:

The Marshall of Rais wife had been heard say that Queen Catherine being desirous to know what should become of her children and who should succeed them, the party which undertook to assure her, let her see a glass, representing a hall, in which either of them made so many turns, as he should reign

[1] IV. iii.

years, that King Henry III making his, the Duke of Guise crossed him like a flash of lightning, after which the Prince of Navarre presented himself and made twenty-two turns and then vanished.

Now there is nothing whatever in Holinshed to suggest the show of kings in *Macbeth*. Holinshed says that Macbeth went to certain wizards and received prophecies from them, but he does not describe any vision; the prophecies given to Macbeth are the reassuring ones—Birnam Wood and the rest—they do not take a visual form and he most certainly is *not* shown the line of his successors.

It looks as if for this truly magnificent conception Shakespeare was again indebted to French history and, as I have already pointed out, I think this particular book of P. Mathieu's invaluable for the light it throws on Shakespeare.

The whole idea of combining the story of the Darnley murder with that of St Bartholomew may seem strange to modern readers, but it had already been done in the Huguenot *Memoires* so often quoted, where the Darnley murder, as told by Buchanan, is inserted into the very midst of the affairs of France. Shakespeare, like the contemporary Huguenots, considers as practically one tragedy the terrible crimes by which the Catholics sought to prevent the Protestant succession in England, and in France; he sees the similarity in their dabbling in witchcraft, the prophecies which terrified them and the prophecies which were, in each case, fulfilled.

Do not let us forget that plots against the Protestant kings were still proceeding in England and France, and that the lives of both Henry IV and James I were held as insecure.

The Catholic conspiracy against the Protestant succession is the leading motive in *Macbeth*.

Shakespeare's chief sources for French history were in all

probability oral tradition. If, as seems now established, he lived for several years in the house of the Huguenot printer, Vautrollier, he would have had every opportunity of meeting French Huguenots and of learning at first hand concerning events in France. The *Memoires* I have quoted (published by Heinrich Wolf, Meidelbourg, 1576) are probably a source for *King Lear* and possibly, though more doubtfully, for *Macbeth*.

The *Inventoire Général de l'Histoire de France*, by J. de Serres, appeared in 1597 and might have been used by Shakespeare. P. V. de Cayet published an account of France in 1605 and portions of de Thou's celebrated narrative also appeared early.

Henry IV's gentlemen did often visit England and it is surely possible that writers like P. Mathieu might come into personal contact with Shakespeare and hear the explanations of his plays from his own lips?

CHAPTER VIII

THE PORTER SCENE—CONCLUSIONS

WE have nearly reached the end of our exposition of *Macbeth* and there remain only a few loose threads to be gathered up.

It has been very generally recognised that the brief scene of the Porter contains, at any rate, one allusion to Gunpowder Plot, and this, as I have pointed out before, is a means by which the play is dated.

It is the allusion:

Faith, here's an equivocator, that could swear in both the scales against either scale; who committed treason enough for God's sake, yet could not equivocate to heaven: O, come in, equivocator[1].

This is plainly an allusion to the trial of Father Garnet to which we find many references in the *State Papers* of 1605. Thus on December 12th, 1605, there is a list of points to be noted in the book of equivocation, suspected to be written by Gerard the Jesuit. The title was altered by Garnet from *A Treatise of Equivocation* to *A Treatise Against Lying and Fraudulent Dissimulation*.

There is a further reference on December 23rd, on the examination of a priest—Richard Andrews:

he thinks the Pope may absolve subjects from allegiance to a heretic king; equivocation is lawful where the right of a questioner is not acknowledged; condemns the Powder Plot as detestable and damnable...has heard of the Book of Equivocation but not seen it.

[1] II. iii.

Another reference occurs on April 28th, 1606: "Exposition and defence of Equivocation by Henry Garnet,"

when asked if it were well to deny on his priesthood that he had written to Greenwell or had conference with Hall, knowing his denial to be false; replied that in his opinion, and that of all the schoolmen, equivocation may be confirmed by oath or sacrament without perjury if just necessity so require.

Garnet's trial dragged on for months and he was finally executed on May 2nd. The *State Papers* record his extreme surprise on being told that he was to die, "he shifts, falters, and equivocates," but "will be hanged without equivocation."

I think it probable, although not certain, that the Porter's speech contains other references to the Gunpowder Plot trials of a somewhat gruesome and "macabre" description. Thus the Porter says: "Here's a farmer, that hanged himself on the expectation of plenty." "Farmer" was the pseudonym under which Garnet had for some time passed.

Another phrase is: "If a man were porter of hell-gate, he should have old turning the key." One of the conspirators was named Robert Keyes[1] and there were several of them racked, another was named Old.

Another phrase is: "Knock, knock; never at quiet! What are you?—But this place is too cold for hell."

Now, in the trial of the Gunpowder Plot conspirators, the intense cold from which they suffered is repeatedly dwelt upon. It was very cold indeed in the vaults where Guy Fawkes was stationed as watchman. Also after their arrest the miserable wretches repeatedly protested against the extreme cold of their dungeons. Thus Silvester Morris—

---

[1] *State Papers*, Domestic Series, November 6th, 1605, February 4th, 1606.

priest—writes to Salisbury (December 1st, 1605) and "asks pity for his extreme sufferings from cold and darkness."

Another phrase is: "I had thought to have let in some of all professions that go the primrose way to the everlasting bonfire."

The Gunpowder Plot conspirators were, of course, executed as traitors; they were dragged on hurdles to the places of execution, put to death by the gruesome and ghastly methods then in vogue and their remains were afterwards burnt in a bonfire; it need hardly be remarked that this was simply to the popular mind a symbol of their fate in the next world.

I can hardly think that so many gruesome and "macabre" resemblances have come by accident. It is, I think, more than probable that the Porter himself is meant as a satire on Guy Fawkes. Guy Fawkes served as the watchman who mounted guard over the cellar, he was found with a huge bunch of keys, it was as intensely cold as he describes it to be, and the Porter's references to himself are almost precisely the language used of Guy Fawkes who is regularly termed "the devil," the "chief devil" and the "devil watchman." "If a man were porter of hell-gate" and "I'll devil-porter it no further."

I cannot help suspecting that what we think of as the intrusions of comedy into Shakespeare's tragedies are not really comedy at all, but simply the tragic grotesque and, when one knows their full meaning, probably the most horrible parts of the play. I showed what I think good reasons for this conclusion with regard to the Grave-digger scene in *Hamlet* and I believe it to be equally true with regard to the Porter-scene in *Macbeth*. I strongly suspect that the Grave-digger and the Porter are made comic on exactly the same principle as Satan and Judas Iscariot were made comic in the mystery-plays—because they could hardly have been tolerated in any other way; they are the tragic grotesque as contrasted with the tragic sublime.

The reader will observe that, just as in the case of *Hamlet*, I find that Macbeth himself is a composite character.

He is certainly not like the Macbeth of Holinshed who is a totally different character, a strong and effective ruler who rules for many years in righteousness before he takes to evil courses.

Shakespeare's Macbeth seems more interesting than any murderer could be in real life and it would appear that Shakespeare has taken from several characters their more interesting traits. Thus in courage and recklessness and terrible audacity Macbeth resembles the elder Bothwell; in his association with witches and evil spirits, in the dreadful glamour of unhallowed prophecy and unhallowed magic practices, Macbeth resembles the younger Bothwell; in his fearful hallucinations, in his anguish and remorse of conscience he resembles Charles IX. He thus becomes what we might term "the ideal murderer," a figure of superhuman horror and superhuman fascination.

Had Shakespeare given us only the elder Bothwell there would have been produced a figure of terrific power and splendid recklessness, but wholly without the dreadful glamour of the supernatural and also a hard, callous man with scarcely any conscience and not deeply interesting because untouched by remorse.

Had he given us only the younger Bothwell there would have been the glamour of the supernatural, but there would have been no consistent plan in crime and once again no remorse of conscience. Had he depicted purely Charles IX we should have had a creature singularly weak in character

and futile in act, tragic only by his dreadful capacity for
moral suffering.

Shakespeare puts all together and the result is one of the
most tragically terrible figures in the world's literature.
Macbeth commits appalling crimes and we are made to feel
their full horror; but he always retains grandeur partly
because of the dreadful courage with which he faces all
things, seen and unseen, and conjures up those powers of
evil who so terrify him, and partly because of his bitter
remorse of conscience which makes him human to the
end.

And surely also Macbeth is the most terrible picture conceivable of an absolutely ruined soul? It is not merely that
he has slain the man who should have been most sacred to
him, that he has violated hallowing sleep and the holy
silence of the night; it is not merely that he has heaped sin
on sin and crime on crime; but he has also penetrated below
and beyond the world itself, into dark reservoirs of unknown
and unfathomable evil which the soul of man dare hardly
dream of exploring and, most tragic of all, he *knows* that
he is ruined and can measure all that his soul might have
been and all that his soul has lost.

Shakespeare certainly, I believe, found the whole of this
in his own time; but I do not believe that he found the
whole of such a terrible sublime in any one human heart.
Hence arises, as many critics have pointed out, a certain
difficulty in the portraiture for it is not easy to reconcile
the hard and resolute side of Macbeth, his great qualities
as a man of action, with the imaginative and neurotic terrors
of his hallucinations. I cannot but believe that Shakespeare is creating something more than man: a figure in
which all the elements are human but in which they are so
combined that the result is superhuman.

As I have said before I find that all Shakespeare's greatest figures, Hamlet, Macbeth, Lear and Prospero, have in them something which is more than human. We must remember that the miracle and mystery plays had dealt with beings greater than life, that Aristotle had taught that the tragic hero was greater than life, that Sir Philip Sidney[1] believed that the poet should be greater than life for God had set man beyond and above nature, "which in nothing hee sheweth so much as in Poetrie; when, with the force of a divine breath, hee bringeth things forth far surpassing her doings."

If Shakespeare deliberately aimed at surpassing nature he was, after all, only in accord with the tradition of his own age.

[1] *Apologie for Poetrie.*

CHAPTER IX

THE PROBLEM OF *KING LEAR*

LET us turn now to a consideration of *King Lear* from the same point of view, asking what the play would mean to a Jacobean audience or to the king himself.

Let us observe, in the first place, that it is a companion play to *Macbeth*, for it was produced about the same time, and that it was written directly for the Court.

"*King Lear*," says Sir Sidney Lee, "was written during 1606 and was produced before the Court at Whitehall on the night of December 26th of the same year. This fact is stated in the Stationers Company's License of November 26th, 1607. It was reprinted in 1608."

Now Shakespeare's treatment of his source in *King Lear* is, as I have pointed out before[1], quite as peculiar as in the case of *Hamlet* and far more peculiar than in the case of *Macbeth*.

I showed that, in the case of *Hamlet*, Shakespeare had turned the Amleth saga completely inside out; he had given the story a different ending, he had completely altered the main problem and the main character; he had added all kinds of new characters and new details and he had completely altered the details he did retain. If it were not for the name *Hamlet* and the circumstance that the hero was a Prince of Denmark, we could hardly have guessed his literary source; we should not even have recognised it had it been put in our hands.

[1] Introduction, also *Hamlet and the Scottish Succession*.

Now in the case of *King Lear* we have as strange a transformation. Let us remember, to begin with, that it was one of those stories with which the Elizabethan public were most thoroughly familiar; it occurs first in Geoffrey of Monmouth's history, it is repeated in Shakespeare's favourite Holinshed, in *The Mirror for Magistrates*, in Spenser's *Faerie Queene*, etc., etc. In all these well-known versions the general outline is similar; King Lear asks his daughters for protestations of affection, is dissatisfied with Cordelia, shares her inheritance between her two sisters, is ill-treated by the two sisters and succoured by Cordelia whose husband—the King of France—comes to the rescue of Lear and restores him to his throne. King Lear reigns happily until his death and Cordelia succeeds him.

Now there are three very important things to notice here.

(1) That the story of King Lear was exceedingly well known: one of the most popular of all Elizabethan tales and that it was taken to be quite authentic and genuine history.

(2) That in all the extant versions the story of King Lear was *not* a tragedy; it ended happily because he himself was restored to the throne and reigned until his death.

(3) That Cordelia triumphed over her sisters, restored her father and herself succeeded. Her story did end in tragedy for she was dethroned and murdered by the wicked sons of her evil sisters; but, so far as her relations to her father were concerned, she was entirely successful.

Now surely Shakespeare has made here the most remarkable changes?

(1) He has completely altered the ending of the story and turned it into a tragedy. This is astonishing because the story was already so well known; it is the more astonishing because the story was regarded as authentic history.

(2) The King of France plays, as we should expect, a very important part in the original story; in Shakespeare's drama he is simply mentioned as the husband who accepts Cordelia in spite of her disinheritance and then passes out of the tale, never to be mentioned again. His wife is imprisoned and put to death; but he never appears, nobody is afraid of his vengeance, nobody even refers to him.

(3) Shakespeare completely alters Cordelia's story for she does not restore her father and does not succeed her father; she falls a victim.

Of course the change in the ending of the story has not escaped the observation of our modern critics; they have explained it, more or less as follows: that Shakespeare, having made Lear suffer such incredible anguish, could not, as it were in any common decency, restore him to his crown; that would be an anti-climax.

I most fully admit that it would. All the same I think they omit the main problem which may be stated thus: If Shakespeare intended to write one of the most terrific of the world's tragedies, as *King Lear* certainly is, why did he choose as his subject a remote king in the bronze age whose story was, in the original, not a tragedy at all but rather a conspicuous example of undeserved good luck?

And the more we examine into the matter the stranger it becomes. In the original version by Geoffrey of Monmouth, Lear and his daughters are all of them more intelligible than in Shakespeare's play and so they are in Holinshed. Thus, Geoffrey of Monmouth does not state that Lear gave away the whole of his kingdom; he reserved a certain portion for himself and, it was in order to gain this portion, that Goneril and Regan made war upon him. Thus Lear and his daughters were all of them more rational; Lear was not so utterly unwise as to strip himself of everything, and Goneril and Regan were not motiveless in their malignancy; they made war upon him for the eminently practical reason of gaining for themselves the remainder of the kingdom.

The same thing is true of Holinshed in whom again the story is much more rational; Holinshed does not say that Lear stripped himself of all; he says that Lear kept his kingdom; but simply appointed his two elder daughters to be his successors, and it was not the daughters themselves, it was their *husbands* who made war upon Lear because he lived to be very old and they were tired of waiting for the inheritance.

Coleridge, in discussing *King Lear*, admitted that certain portions of the tale were improbable; but he pleaded that it was an old story, to which the audience were accustomed and therefore, being accustomed, would not note the improbabilities which were, as our modern idiom would have put it, "given." This is certainly true of the love-test and of the anger against Cordelia; but the other improbabilities were not in the original story and were added by Shakespeare himself. In the original tale the daughters have, at any rate, a motive and in Shakespeare's favourite Holinshed it is the husbands who start the injustice. But Shakespeare gives Lear's daughters no motive whatever; instead he makes them hate him with an intensely vindictive hatred. Now why? A modern poet—Mr Gordon Bottomley—has felt the difficulty so acutely that he has written a drama in which he tells us how, at a previous period of his life, Lear had ill-treated the mother of Goneril.

Well! Mr Gordon Bottomley certainly rationalises the story but one must observe that there is nothing whatever in the text to support him; Lear calls himself an "old, kind father, whose frank heart gave you all" and everything in the text confirms him.

A quite ordinary greed is, I repeat, the main motive in the historical sources; but the Lear of Shakespeare's story has given all, and the main motive of Shakespeare's drama is thus a marble-hearted, inexplicable, inexpressible ingratitude.

And just as Shakespeare robs Lear's daughters of their only intelligible motive so he makes Lear himself much more unintelligible. The Lear of Geoffrey of Monmouth was, apart from the love-test, very reasonably prudent; he did retain a certain portion of his kingdom for himself. So also the Lear of Holinshed, Shakespeare's favourite source, was very reasonably prudent for he simply appointed his daughters to be his heirs after his death and a portion was given them as earnest

betwixt whome (i.e. the Dukes who had married them) he willed and ordained that his land should be divided after his death, and the one half thereof immediately should be assigned to them in hand.

Moreover, when the daughters ill-treat him, he very sensibly goes to France in search of help and obtains it.

But Shakespeare's Lear is robbed of these reasonable motives; he strips himself of *all*, he retains nothing except the empty honour of his hundred knights; when he is turned out by his daughters it never occurs to him, as it does at once to Holinshed's Lear, to go and ask help from a strong son-in-law who can be rewarded by Cordelia's inheritance. The Lear of Holinshed knew at once that he had that card (a successful one, as it proved) to play; but Shakespeare's Lear shows an utter rashness and an utter helplessness; he trusts himself, stripped of all, into the hands of these women who call him "father" and flatter him boundlessly; but who hate him with a deadly hate.

A tragic and incredible folly and a blind and overwhelming trust in the wicked are the main characteristics of the play and neither of them were anything like so strong in the original story.

Moreover, Shakespeare increases the improbability with regard even to the rejection scene. The original Lear repudiated Cordelia but he did not repudiate also his most faithful servant; there is no "Kent" in Geoffrey of Monmouth or in Holinshed; it is reserved for Shakespeare to double the improbability by making the faithful friend and servant and councillor cast out with the daughter.

Shakespeare gives us one improbability heaped upon another. Why does he make the conduct of all the principal characters in the play so profoundly irrational, making it irrational even where, in his source, it was quite reasonable?

Moreover, the same curious treatment of the material is manifest in other directions. Thus Shakespeare has not drawn his material only from the Geoffrey of Monmouth and Holinshed tale of Lear; the story of Gloucester and his sons was taken from an entirely different source in Sidney's *Arcadia*. As we have seen the story of Lear was accepted as quite genuine history by the Elizabethans. The *Arcadia* was a pastoral romance. Surely Shakespeare is once again acting in a very extraordinary manner! Why should he take this tale which is regarded as authentic history and put into its midst a tale, also very well known, from a work of fiction. Suppose, for instance, that in writing *Strafford* Browning introduced the character of Waverley, whom everybody knows to be not a historical character at all, but a hero of Sir Walter Scott's. Would it not seem needlessly strange?

It is the same problem as the story of Duff and Donwald

inserted into the middle of *Macbeth*, only in more acute form, for here the inserted material is not chronicle history at all.

Moreover the new material has one characteristic in which it resembles the old for Shakespeare has altered the ending. In the story of Gloucester and his sons as told by Sidney (it is in the *Arcadia* the story of the blind king of Paphlagonia) the blind king himself succumbs to his grief and dies; the two brothers become reconciled and the wicked one repents. Shakespeare, on the contrary, has made Gloucester survive his injuries and come to a happy restoration; but he has not allowed the reconciliation between the brothers for the evil brother perishes by the forces he has himself set in motion.

The story of Gloucester makes, as many critics have pointed out, a curious replica of the story of Lear; they are like the repetition of similar themes in music. Shakespeare often employs under-plots; but he has nowhere else employed an under-plot which is so close a replica of the main plot.

Mr Bradley, we may remember, compares *King Lear* to Beethoven's fifth symphony, and the "repeat" of a motive so grand and so tragic really does convey an almost musical effect.

Sidney's *Arcadia* was sometimes believed to have been a political allegory. Now, so far as my work has gone, I have not been able to find any English interpretation, but there is what looks like a French interpretation of the story of Gloucester and that, as I have said, occurs in Pierre Mathieu's *Deplorable Death of Henry IV of France*.

I will deal with it more fully later but the sum and substance comes to this: the blind father is France and the blindness is symbolic of the blind and rash acts of that country; of the two sons the younger illegitimate son so treacherous towards his father is Henry of Guise; the legitimate son treated with such harsh injustice and so nobly devoted is Henry of Navarre.

Now here again we surely have some very remarkable facts?

In the first place P. Mathieu's allegory is undoubtedly a life of Henry IV of France. In the second place a portion of it does undoubtedly bear the closest possible resemblance to the Gloucester part of *King Lear*. But, if Gloucester is to be interpreted as France, if Edmund is the Duke of Guise and if Edgar is Henry of Navarre, who then is Lear and who are his daughters?

What, in short, is to be the interpretation of *King Lear* as a whole?

It is this question which I intend to answer or to attempt to answer in the following pages.

Here I will only point out that, if *King Lear* really is a political play, in which the nations themselves are protagonists and in which ungrateful children mean the factions of a civil war, tearing their fatherland to pieces[1], then we can understand both the supreme greatness of *King Lear* as a play and also the alterations which Shakespeare makes in the original; for he certainly could not here (just as he could not in the case of *Hamlet*) find any previous material that would fit his political ideas in all their details.

Also we understand the terrible depth of the tragedy in *King Lear* and the passion which the subject itself excites in Shakespeare and which is so different from the languid antiquarian interest of most of his contemporaries.

---

[1] This metaphor is exceedingly common in the French historians. See also D'Aubigné's *Les Tragiques*.

CHAPTER X

KING LEAR AND THE DARNLEY MURDER

KING LEAR may be regarded as almost a companion piece to *Macbeth*. As we have seen the general estimate of its date is that it was written some time in 1606 and produced before the Court at Whitehall.

Now I have shown already what the "complex" was in the minds of Shakespeare's audience at that date. The Gunpowder Plot was the great event of contemporary history; it had terrified the nation to a degree very difficult to realise to-day. It was compared by the king himself to his father's murder and by the populace to the massacre of St Bartholomew; it was supposed to be the work of the same Catholic League which had planned both the previous crimes and which had produced or which had, at any rate, been a main agent in producing the Civil War in France. French Catholics blamed the French Protestants for the division of their kingdom and the Civil Wars. It was equally inevitable that the English Protestants should blame the Guises and the Catholic League.

King Lear was written at a time when this same "complex" of emotions was dominant in the mind of the king and in the minds of his audience; it would therefore be perfectly natural that *King Lear* should appeal to this "complex" of emotions and I am convinced that it does.

In studying Buchanan's *Detection of the Doings of Mary, Queen of Scots* and the appended *Oration* for the purpose of their relations to *Hamlet*, I became convinced that they were also sources for a large part of *King Lear*, and that many of the incidents and circumstances in that play which had no relation to the original story were to be found in the story of Darnley. A further examination of contemporary documents only confirmed me strongly in this idea.

The parallels with the Darnley murder can, I think, be grouped mainly under the following heads:

(1) Darnley was supposed by contemporaries to have been led to his doom mainly by false professions of affection and by his own excessive credulity. It was the special heinousness of Mary's crime against him in the eyes of Buchanan and the author of the *Oration* that she employed professions of her own affection to ensnare him to his doom.

(2) Darnley was very rash and credulous in deserting all his own friends and placing himself entirely in the power of those who were false to him.

(3) Darnley's murder is repeatedly termed a "parricide" by Buchanan and others because a husband stood in the same relation to his wife as a father to a child.

(4) A great conflict had proceeded between Mary and Darnley over the title of "king." He wished to have the full rights of the crown matrimonial and complained that his authority was only a shadow. Mary's determination to exclude him from power brought the tragedy to a climax.

(5) Darnley's great faults were pride and haughtiness and a tendency to break into furious rages.

(6) Darnley was accused of egregious folly by his enemies and many contemporaries record that his opponents termed him "The Fool" and "The Boy," but especially the fool.

(7) Buchanan and the *Oration* accuse Mary of taking away the king's servants, of forbidding her own servants to obey the king, of commanding the ambassadors not to speak with him, of denying him money even for the necessities of life and of making him a beggar and an outlaw.

(8) Buchanan and the *Oration* accuse Mary of denying the king house-room and of thrusting him naked out of doors into desert-places and on heaths.

(9) Buchanan and the *Oration* accuse Mary of compelling the king to take refuge in a ruinous house, tumble-down and ill-furnished, and to consort only with beggars.

(10) Darnley, having a strong suspicion of his impending fate, tried to escape to France but the attempt was frustrated.

(11) Buchanan and the *Oration* declare that the king was repeatedly the subject of the most bitter humiliations, Mary taking a delight in insulting him for the sake of insults.

(12) His body was found after his death in an open field, close by the body of his servant, both naked. There is a picture of this in the Plan of the Darnley Murder kept in the Record Office.

(13) Bothwell himself had the unparalleled impudence to assert that the king was killed in a thunderstorm and that either he himself in his madness or the lightning had stripped his clothes from him.   (Melville's *Memoirs*.)

It will be obvious that these things, if substantiated (and I have already named the main sources), offer far closer parallels to Shakespeare's play than anything in the Geoffrey of Monmouth or Holinshed *Chronicles*. How many, we may enquire, of the above parallels are to be found in the old tale of Lear?

(1) Of course is similar in both. The Lear of the *Chronicle Histories* is certainly lured on by false professions of affection. Even here, however, Shakespeare's drama is far closer to the Darnley story for, as I have repeatedly pointed out, the original tale of Lear is not a tragedy at all, whereas the Darnley murder is one of the most terrible tragedies in the annals of Scotland.

(2) Here also Shakespeare is closer to the Darnley story for the Lear of the *Chronicles* does not strip himself entirely; he reserves some security. But it is one of the main points of Buchanan's narrative that the unhappy victim has *complete* confidence and abandons himself *entirely*.

(3) There is no mention of any "parricide" in the original story of *King Lear*, and could not be as the old king is not killed, but regains his throne. The Darnley murder is termed a "parricide," and Shakespeare's *King Lear* is also a parricide and a very terrible one, too.

(4) There is no quarrel over the title of "king" in Shakespeare's sources; the real grievance there is the fact that Lear does possess actual power; he has retained a good portion of the kingdom himself. Darnley, however, was full of grief over his mere shadow of power and this is the case with Shakespeare's Lear.

(5) No stress is laid in any of Shakespeare's sources on the excessive pride and haughtiness of Lear; he wishes to keep the insignia of his rank as he has a right to keep them, but that is all.

Shakespeare's Lear, on the other hand, is like Darnley, excessively haughty.

(6) The folly of Lear is sufficiently obvious in the old tale in the egregious circumstances of the love-test, but it is not otherwise dwelt upon. It was reserved for Shakespeare, by means of the biting image of the Fool, to keep Lear's folly continually in his mind. Here again he resembles the Darnley story, for that unhappy prince did most fully realise his folly and most deeply repent of it.

(7) Nothing is said of the Lear of the *Chronicles* being reduced to absolute beggary or of the nobles being forbidden to speak to him. These things occur in Shakespeare's drama and in the Darnley story but in them only.

(8) Nothing is said of the Lear of the *Chronicles* being thrust out into a "desert-place" or a solitude. Darnley, however, is thrust out into solitude, into desert-places and among the "craggy mountains" of Scotland, and Shakespeare's Lear is thrust out on a "heath."

(9) Nothing is said in the *Chronicles* of Lear being compelled to inhabit a ruinous house and to consort with beggars. These things happen, however, to Darnley and they happen to Shakespeare's Lear.

(10) The Lear of the *Chronicles* made his escape success-

fully to France. Darnley tried to escape to France but was foiled and Shakespeare's Lear is on his way to Dover when he also is cut off by his enemies.

(11) Humiliating insults are offered both to the Lear of the *Chronicles* and to Shakespeare's Lear. The humiliations offered to Darnley, however, included calculated insults from menials and in this again Shakespeare's Lear resembles him for this episode does not occur in the *Chronicles*.

(12) In no previous version is it said that Lear and his companion either stripped themselves naked or were stripped naked; but this certainly occurs as a detail in the Darnley murder, and it occurs in Shakespeare's play. In the *Chronicles* no mention whatever is made of any nakedness in a thunderstorm.

I will now proceed to deal with the parallels at greater length.

Flattery is used as a means to entrap Lear; Goneril and Regan flatter him grossly and coarsely and it is Lear's susceptibility to flattery which is the cause of his ruin. The same thing happened in the case of the unhappy Darnley. Thus we read in the *Burghley State Papers*, 1568, in an "Abstract of Matters Shewed to the Queen's Majesty's Commissioners by the Scots":

> She wrote to Bothwell from Glasco, how she flattered her said Husband, to obtain her Purpose.
> ...Finally she wrote to Bothwell that according to her Commission, she would bring the man with her, praying him to work wisely...and specially to make good watch that the Bird escaped not out of the Cage.

We may compare this with Lear's phrase which seems so bitterly ironic where it comes in the play[1]:

> We two alone will sing like birds i' the cage.

[1] v. iii.

Melville in his *Memoirs* also speaks of Darnley's susceptibility to flattery as being one of the chief causes of his ruin:

It was a great pity to see that good young prince casten off,
who failed rather for lack of good counsel and experience, than
of evil will. It appeared to be his destiny to like better of
flatterers and evil company, than of plain speeches and good
men.

Again the complete confidence with which Darnley trusted
himself into the hands of Mary startled and even shocked
contemporaries.

The *Oration* says: "She goeth to her husband, she kisseth
him, she giveth him a ring for pledge ɩf her love," and again,

How much greater tokens the queen showed of reconciled
affection, so much the more cruelty did every man in his heart
preconceive of all her intentions.

Darnley's murder is repeatedly termed a parricide. Belleforest, in the work already alluded to as having possibly
given suggestions for Macbeth, *Histoire de Marie Royne
d'Escosse*, 1572, refers to the crime as a "parricide." He
speaks of the real offenders trying to cast the blame on
others: "toutesfois ils pensent innocenter leur malice en
saisant le proces à ceux qu'ils ont faits parricides."

Adam Blackwood, in his version published in 1587, terms
the murder a "parricide."

The *Oration* repeatedly dwells on the awful wickedness of
this deed because it is a double violation of the two most
sacred things on earth, matrimony and royal majesty.

Whosoever I do not say hurteth the king that is the true
image of God upon earth, but slayeth him with strange and
unwonted sort of cruelty...seemeth he not as much as in him
lyeth, to have a desire to pull God out of heaven.

Now in the original *Chronicle* tale of Lear we have nothing
of this terrific solemnity, this sense of the greatest of all

human duties violated and all human sacraments broken; but surely this is just the sense that is predominant in Shakespeare's *King Lear*?

We may compare with the passage above Lear's own words[1]:

> O heavens,
> If you do love old men, if your sweet sway
> Allow obedience, if yourselves are old,
> Make it your cause; send down, and take my part!

The metaphors used in the one case often closely suggest those in the other. Thus Crawford in his *Declaration*[2] said:

> He would never think that she who was his own proper flesh would do him hurt....My opinion was she took him more like a prisoner than like a husband. He answered he thought little less himself save the confidence he had in her promise only. Yet he would put himself in her hands though she would cut his throat and besought God to be judge over them both.

Now here we surely have remarkable similarities. There is the identity of flesh as when Lear says[3]:

> Is it not as this mouth should tear this hand
> For lifting food to 't?

and again,

> Is it the fashion, that discarded fathers
> Should have thus little mercy on their flesh?
> Judicious punishment! 'twas this flesh begot
> Those pelican daughters[4].

We observe also the fact that Darnley is taken prisoner by Mary much as Lear is taken prisoner by Goneril and Regan.

The title of "king" was a matter of great significance in Darnley's history.

---

[1] II. iv. [2] *Scottish State Papers.*
[3] III. iv. [4] See also Chap. XIV.

We might observe incidentally that the Goneril of Shakespeare's play is the wife of the Duke of Albany, and this was actually the title that Mary, Queen of Scots, would hold from her husband for Darnley had been created Duke of Albany as Holinshed records of the year 1563: "In the month of July the lord Darnley, earl of Ross, was made Duke of Albany."

In the first ardour of her affection Mary gave Darnley the title of King of Scotland, without consulting her Parliament, a circumstance which greatly exasperated that body. Thus on July 28th, 1563, the day before the marriage, Darnley was proclaimed King by the Queen's commandment at the market cross of Edinburgh. In the early days of the marriage his name "Henricus Rex" was placed before hers on royal seals to be affixed to proclamations and other documents; but in 1565 both Buchanan and Holinshed note that the order of the names in writings and on the seal was altered while the use of Darnley's seal was entrusted to Rizzio who was terribly insolent to him.

"The order of the names," says Holinshed "in writings and protests was altered (in 1565); the king's name had hitherto been placed before the Queen's, now it was altered and David the secretary had a stamp of the king's name which he affixed when he liked."

Mary, in fact, gave the real authority and true supremacy in her counsels to Rizzio instead of to her husband and this fact was counted as a special outrage by all Darnley's defenders.

We will compare later this prominent position assigned to Rizzio with the position assigned by Shakespeare to Oswald, the base steward of Goneril, a person who does not appear in the *Chronicles*, but who is introduced by Shakespeare as a domineering and contemptible menial given authority over the powerless king precisely as Darnley's friends represent Rizzio as a domineering and contemptible fellow given full insolent authority over the powerless king of Scotland. And, just as in *King Lear* the intrusions of Oswald cause aggravated mischief between Lear and Goneril so did the intrusions of Rizzio cause aggravated mischief between the queen and Darnley.

Darnley all the more eagerly reached after the reality of power and felt all the more bitterly discontented with its shadow. In 1566, Holinshed records, Murray's friends persuaded Darnley to stay the Parliament and to summon Murray back on condition that:

he (i.e. Darnley) be made and crowned king of Scotland absolutely, and the queen so to have less to do with the government afterwards, where through he agreed with them.

Darnley not only desired the title of king and clung to the title, but he could not bear to be deposed from power; he was particularly proud and haughty and very violent in his anger so as to excite positive terror at times in those surrounding him.

Additional passages bearing on these circumstances may be quoted.

Thus Randolph writes to Leicester, July 31st, 1565:

this Queen is now become a married wife, and her husband, the self-same day of his marriage, made a king....

His words to all men, against whom he conceiveth any displeasure how unjust so ever to be, so proud and spiteful, that rather he seemeth a monarch of the world than he that not long since we have seen and known the Lord Darnley.

We may compare this with the pride and anger shown by Lear and with the accusations brought against him by Regan and others[1]:

> O the blest gods! So will you wish on me
> When the rash mood is on,

---

[1] II. iv.

and with his own claim of superb pride when Gloucester asks:

> Is 't not the king?

and he answers[1]:

> Ay, every inch a king:
> When I do stare, see how the subject quakes.

Darnley, as a matter of fact, never had more than the shadow of power and even that soon disappeared.

On December 25th, 1565, Randolph writes to Cecil: "A while ago there was nothing but 'King' and 'Queen,' his majestie and hers, now the 'queen's husband' is most common."

We may compare this with the anger of Lear at his subjection[2]:

LEAR. Who am I, sir?
Osw. My lady's father.
LEAR. "My lady's father"! my lord's knave: you whoreson dog!

Darnley thoroughly resented his position of subjection and devoted his best energies to protests.

Randolph writes to Cecil, January 16th, 1566:

> I cannot tell what mislikings of late there hath been between her Grace and her husband; he presses earnestly for the matrimonial crown, which she is loth hastily to grant, but willing to keep somewhat in store until she knows how well he is worthy to enjoy such a sovereignty.

It was this attitude of tutelage, of being kept in subjection and put on his good behaviour which, from the beginning, infuriated the proud heart of Darnley. It is the shadow of power possessed by him which is so bitter to Lear and it is the attitude of tutelage adopted by his daughters which he so detests and abominates.

---

[1] IV. vi.   [2] I. iv.

We may compare the Fool's speech to Lear[1]:

Thou art an O without a figure: I am better than thou art now; I am a fool, thou art nothing,

and again when Lear asks:

Who is it that can tell me who I am?

and the Fool replies: "Lear's shadow."

Lear raves: "by the marks of sovereignty, knowledge and reason, I should be false persuaded I had daughters," and the Fool responds:

Which they will make an obedient father.

At every step his weakness and impotence are driven home as in the dreadful speech of Regan[2]:

I pray you, father, being weak, seem so.

Another interesting letter is that of Randolph, March 6th, 1566, when we hear both that Darnley is desiring the crown matrimonial and that he considers he has received intolerable treatment at Mary's hands.

Somewhat we are sure you have heard of divers discords and jars between this Queen and her husband, partly for that she hath refused him the crown matrimonial, partly for that he hath assured knowledge of such usage of herself, as altogether is intolerable to be borne.

Darnley, of course, suspected Mary of the basest sensuality and it is notable that this is one of the terrible charges brought by Lear against Goneril:

The fitchew, nor the soilèd horse, goes to 't
With a more riotous appetite.
Down from the waist they are Centaurs,
Though women all above:
But to the girdle do the gods inherit,
Beneath is all the fiends';
    *   *   * Give me an ounce of civet, good apothecary,
to sweeten my imagination: there 's money for thee[3].

---

[1] I. iv.   [2] II. iv.   [3] See also Chap. XIV.

The atrocious language heaped on Mary by her wretched husband seems to have been quite equal to this. No such accusation is brought against the Goneril of the old story or even hinted at.

The whole of this part of Darnley's story almost exactly resembles the main position in *King Lear*; it is that of a man who has the name indeed of king but who has hardly even the shadow of power, who feels his position acutely, who is continually but vainly endeavouring to assert himself, who thinks himself dreadfully ill-treated by the very person who had previously lavished on him all possible professions of affection and who is not merely ill-treated, but incessantly insulted, a person, moreover, who is so excessively proud and haughty that his best friends continually deprecate his pride.

Thus M. de Croc writes to the Archbishop of Glasgow, December 2nd, 1566:

I do not expect, upon several accounts, any good understanding between them, unless God effectually put to His hand. The first is, the King will never humble himself as he ought; the other is the Queen can't perceive any one nobleman speaking with the King, but presently she suspects some contrivance among them.

We may compare this with Goneril's incessant jealousy of Lear's gentlemen and her determination to get rid of them[1].

Adam Blackwood (writing 1587) makes Murray the villain of the piece and says that he especially warned Mary against Darnley's pride; he told the queen:

that he would overthrow himself if her Majesty held not the bridle, and that the crown which he demanded would be the ruin of them both if she agreed with him; she did well to keep her sovereignty with herself.

[1] I. iii, iv.

...he blamed his (i.e. Darnley's) pride that he was so insolent as to aspire to have the title of King of Scots and abuse the Queen as if she were a slave; that his insolencie was intolerable, not only in regard of her Majesty, but also of all the nobility; that it was necessary to bridle it.

Darnley carried his insolence so far that he would sometimes strike messengers. So on May 21st, 1566, Randolph writes to Leicester:

he is grown so proud that to all honest men he is intolerable; and almost forgetful of his duty to her already....What shall be judged of him that for bringing a message from the queen that was to his discontentment would with his dagger have slain the messenger.

Now accusations of this kind are brought against Lear. Goneril says[1]:

Gon. Did my father strike my gentleman for chiding of his fool?
Osw. Ay, madam.
Gon. By day and night he wrongs me: every hour
  He flashes into one gross crime or other
  That sets us all at odds.

We may compare also Randolph to Cecil[2]:

Darnley keeps his chamber...in words I hear he is stout, by some deeds also he has shown what his will is if his power were equal to his furious passions. With his dagger he would have struck the Justice Clerk that brought him word that the creation of his being duke was deferred for a time.

This is very like Lear who certainly shows terrific passions and at the same time impotence[3]:

  I will have such revenges on you both,
  That all the world shall—I will do such things,—
  What they are, yet I know not; but they shall be
  The terrors of the earth.

Rage and impotence were indeed the leading character-

---

[1] I. iii. [2] *Calendar of Scottish State Papers.* [3] II. iv.

istics of Darnley just as they are of Lear; nothing like this is found in the literary source.

So also we may quote Randolph to Leicester, June 3rd:

> The hatred towards him (i.e. Darnley) and his house is marvellous great, his pride intolerable, his words not to be borne but where no man dare speak again.
> ...The passions and furies I hear say he will sometimes be in, are strange to believe....They find nothing but God will send him a short end.

Here again we have the closest possible resemblances to Lear whose passions and furies are indeed things "strange to believe" and who does use "words not to be borne" as in his taunts to Goneril, "Degenerate bastard," "Detested kite[1]," and the rest.

As for accusations of unruly behaviour Goneril brings them continually against Lear and his household[2]:

> Not only, sir, this your all-licens'd fool,
> But other of your insolent retinue
> Do hourly carp and quarrel...
> I would you would make use of your good wisdom,
> Whereof I know you are fraught; and put away
> These dispositions, which of late transform you
> From what you rightly are.

The egregious folly of Darnley was, of course, one of the chief charges made against him by his enemies, and admitted reluctantly even by his friends. In the confession of the Laird of Ormistown concerning the murder we read that

> it was thought expedient and most profitable for the commonwealth, by the whole nobility and lords undersubscribed, that such a young fool and proud tyrant should not reign nor bear rule over them.

So also we read in Melville's *Memoirs*: "I met her Majesty coming from Dunbar to Haddington...she lamented unto

[1] I. iv.   [2] I. iv.

me the king's folly, unthankfulness and misbehaviour." He did his best to persuade her to reconciliation, but "I could perceive nothing but a great grudge that she had in her heart."

Shakespeare has introduced into his *King Lear* the enigmatic and wonderful figure of the fool concerning whom even modern critics have been found to say that he seems like a living embodiment of Lear's folly. He is termed sometimes "a fool" and sometimes "a boy," and he does seem to be like a symbol or a detached personality of that second self in Lear which had ruined Lear[1].

The figure of the fool appears to me a plain piece of symbolism and a very grim and terrible one, too.

---

[1] So in *The Tempest* it would appear that the figure of Ariel is a detached portion of the personality of Henry IV—a sort of outward sign of his swiftly-acting genius. See Appendix B.

CHAPTER XI

KING LEAR AND THE DARNLEY MURDER (cont.)

ANOTHER important matter to notice is the way in which Lear is deprived of his servants, treated with studied insolence by the servants of his daughter and reduced to beggary.

This again closely resembles the history of Darnley whose defenders made continual complaint of the way in which he was deprived of his attendants, of the studied insolence of Mary's servants, especially of Rizzio whose part is very closely akin to that played by Oswald, and also of the extremity of the poverty to which the unhappy Darnley was reduced.

Thus in Crawford's deposition[1] concerning the murder we read: "He (i.e. Darnley) had neither the wherewithal to sustain himself nor his servants."

We read in the *Spanish State Papers*, January 18th, 1567:

The displeasure of the queen of Scotland with her husband is carried so far...that she shows him no affection. They tell me even that she has tried to take away some of his servitors, and for some time past finds him no money for his ordinary expenditure.

In the *Scottish State Papers*, April 5th, 1566, we find Randolph writing to Cecil:

The King of all others is in the worst case, for the Queen has no trust in him nor the people...the Queen is determined the house of Lennox shall be as poor as ever it was.

[1] Goodall.

David Chalmers in his *Chronicle of the Kings of Scotland*, published in 1572, says that at the baptism of the child (i.e. James)

> there was small regard had to the mounting of the King, whereby he wanting such things as became a king at such a solemn time, he is commanded not to come in presence of the ambassadors and the nobility were commanded not to obey him.

> The king, seeing himself despised, and his enemy Bothwell preferred to him, rode away to his father at Glasgow.

Now we have a precisely similar situation in *King Lear* where the nobility are commanded not to obey the king, and his enemy—Oswald—is preferred before him.

Goneril says to Oswald[1]:

> If you come slack of former services,
> You shall do well; the fault of it I'll answer,

and again[2]:

> And let his knights have colder looks among you;
> What grows of it, no matter; advise your fellows so:
> I would breed from hence occasions, and I shall.

We have also the conversation between Lear and the Knight:

> LEAR. Why came not the slave back to me, when I called him?
> KNIGHT. Sir, he answered me in the roundest manner, he would not.
> LEAR. He would not!
> KNIGHT. My lord, I know not what the matter is; but, to my judgment, your highness is not entertained with that ceremonious affection as you were wont: there's a great abatement of kindness appears as well in the general dependants, as in the duke himself also and your daughter.

[1] I. iii.   [2] I. iii.

The scorn and contempt heaped on Darnley were, in fact, commonplaces; thus on October 15th, 1566, de Croc wrote from Jedburgh:

there is not one person in all this kingdom, from the highest to the lowest, that regards him (i.e. Darnley) any further than is agreeable to the queen.

This corresponds precisely with Lear who is so much of an outcast that he has no companion but the Fool; if this means, as I think it does, that the unhappy titular king had only his own folly to befriend him, we can see the infinite pathos and bitterness of Shakespeare's irony.

The most important parallels, however, are to be found in Buchanan's *Detection* and in the appended *Oration*, both books which were readily available as sources to Shakespeare, which would certainly be well known to James I since the author of the first was his own tutor, and which were well known to the general public.

"You," says the *Oration* to Mary, "drove away his servants that should have defended his life; you thrust him out, naked, alone, unarmed, among thieves to be slain; when in all this miserable state of your husband, your adulterer dwelt in your palace...your poor husband was barred from all company of the nobility, his servants forbidden to come at him or sent away from him and thrust away into solitary desert for a laughing-stock."

Now here we surely have the closest possible parallels to Lear? They hardly could be closer. We have Darnley thrust out, "naked, alone and unarmed." So is Lear thrust out alone; so is he unarmed; so is he naked in the storm for he tears off his clothes[1]. So are Lear's servants sent away in the dreadful competition in cruelty between the two

---

[1] III. iv.

sisters when they beat him down to fifty knights; then to five and twenty and then to none at all[1]:

GON.   Hear me, my lord:
            What need you five and twenty, ten, or five,
            To follow in a house, where twice so many
            Have a command to tend you?
REG.   What need one?

and Lear's bitter reply:

LEAR. O, reason not the need: our basest beggars
            Are in the poorest thing superfluous:
            Allow not nature more than nature needs,
            Man's life is cheap as beast's.

So, again, is Lear cast out into a desert place, "a heath," and so does he feel bitterly that he is a "mocking-stock[2]."

LEAR. Arraign her first; 'tis Goneril. I here take my oath before this honourable assembly, she kicked the poor king her father.

And again:

            The little dogs and all,
        Tray, Blanch, and Sweet-heart, see, they bark at me.

We may compare also Crawford's deposition:

He presumed not to come in her presence till he knew her mind, for the sharp things she spoke of him to his servant—Robert Cunningham....

I answered his lordship would the secrets of every creature's heart were written on their face.

We may compare this with Cordelia's words to Goneril and Regan:

                    I know what you are:
        *   *   *   *   *   *
        Time shall unfold what plaited cunning hides[3].

[1] II. iv.   [2] III. vi.   [3] I. i.

Crawford's deposition continues:

He said in reply to her, she was the cause of his sickness and " Ye asked me what I meant by the cruelties specified in my letters?...it proceeded of you only that will not accept my offers and repentance....God knows how I am punished for making my god of you and for having no other thought but of you...necessity compelled me to keep it in my breast and brought me in such melancholy as ye see me in..." he had nothing to sustain himself or his servants as she knew as well as he.

Here again we have the closest parallels to Lear. Lear also is reduced to sickness and to the deepest melancholy by his daughter's unkindness; he refuses to seek shelter from the storm,

> where the greater malady is fix'd,
> The lesser is scarce felt[1].

So did Lear long to be with his daughters and desire only their kindness, so was he punished for making his gods of them.

Buchanan and the *Oration* accuse Mary of cherishing her adulterer when she had thrust Darnley out of doors.

The *Detection* says,

As in making of her marriage, her lightness was very headlong and rash, so suddenly followed either inward repentance, or at least outward token of change of affection without any cause appearing. For where beforetime the king was not only neglected but also not honourably used, at length began open hatred to break out against him, specially in that winter when he went to Peebles with small train even too mean for the degree of a private man...as commanded away into a corner far from counsel and knowledge of public affairs. Neither is it necessary to put in writing these things, which, as they were then a spectacle noted of all men's eyes, so now as a fresh image they remain imprinted on all men's hearts.

Here again we have the closest parallels; we have the

---

[1] III. iv.

causeless change from the warmest professions of affection to the bitterest hate, a change on whose utter unreason Buchanan specially insists just as Shakespeare insists on it in the case of Lear; there is once more the dwelling on the small and mean train of servants unworthy of a king or even of a private man but such as Goneril and Regan thought good enough for Lear; there is the fact˙ that Darnley, like Lear, is commanded away "into a corner." There is also the statement that these things were in themselves "a spectacle"; the very word suggests material for a drama.

Buchanan proceeds:

> After that she was delivered of her child, though she court-eously entertained all others, yet as oft as word was brought her, that the king was come to see her, both she and her company so framed their speech and countenance, as if they seemed to fear nothing more than that the king should not perceive that they loathed him and that his coming and presence were displeasant to them all. On the other side Bothwell was all in all, he alone was governor of all her counsels and all her affairs.

Here again is a situation which corresponds in the closest details. The attitude of Goneril and Regan to Lear might be summed up in Buchanan's words: "They seemed to fear nothing more than that the king should not perceive that they loathed him." The open and obvious insolence with which Goneril and her train treat Lear is exactly like the open and obvious insolence with which, according to Buchanan, Mary treated Darnley.

As for Bothwell, the adulterer, being governor of all Mary's counsels and her affairs this again closely resembles the relation of Goneril to Edmund. Lear, in fact, is subordinated both to Oswald and to Edmund, just as Darnley was subordinated to Rizzio and to Bothwell.

The old *Chronicle* story of Lear contains the parts *neither* of Oswald *nor* of Edmund. The general outline of the tale of Gloucester is derived, as is always acknowledged, from Sidney's *Arcadia*, but this contains, be it noted, no parallel whatever for the relations of Goneril and Edmund which are Shakespeare's addition and Shakespeare's alone.

Buchanan narrates later how the king followed the queen to Aloe Castle:

> The king...followed after with all the haste that he possibly could...and there overtook her in purpose and hoping there to be in her company and to enjoy the loving fellowship of marriage...being scarcely suffered to tarry there a few hours, while his men and horses baited, he was enforced to get him away in haste again and pain of further peril. As for herself she pastimed there in more than princely or rather unprincely licentiousness....
>
> There how coyly, yet how loftily and disdainfully she behaveth to the king what needeth it to be rehearsed....
>
> In the meantime (i.e. while she commits adultery with Bothwell) the king commanded out of sight, with injuries and miseries banished from her, kept himself close with a few servants at Sterling. For alas what else should he do? He could not creep into any piece of grace with the queen, nor could get so much as to maintain his daily necessary expenses to find his few servants and his horses: and finally with brawlings lightly rising from every small trifle and quarrels usually picked he was chased out of her presence.
>
> Yet his heart obstinately fixed in loving her, could not be restrained, but he must needs come back to Edinburgh of purpose with all kinds of serviceable humbleness to get some entry into her former favour, and to recover the kind society of marriage. Who once again with most dishonourable disdain excluded, once again returneth from whence he came, there as in solitary desert to bewail his woefull miseries.

Once again we have the exact situation; the parallels are, beyond comparison, closer than anything to be found in

Shakespeare's so-called literary sources. We have something not found in any of the literary sources, i.e. the king's pursuit of Mary in affection and longing for her love. So does Lear ride in search of Regan.

We have the fact that Darnley is hardly "suffered to tarry there a few hours" which exactly expresses what happens to Lear in the case of Regan, because he has been there only the briefest space when the quarrel arises and he is (in Buchanan's phrase) "enforced to get him away in haste again." There is also the "unprincely licentiousness" which is certainly the characteristic of Goneril no less than of Mary. The lofty and disdainful behaviour is certainly exhibited to Lear by both Goneril and Regan and excites Lear's frenzied rage[1]:

> How now, daughter! what makes that frontlet on? Methinks you are too much of late i' the frown.

And also with Regan[2]:

> The king would speak with Cornwall; the dear father
> Would with his daughter speak, commands her service.

Exactly similar again is the fact that Goneril gives herself up to her adultery with Edmund, that Lear is commanded "out of sight," that he remains with "only a few servants."

Buchanan's words "with brawlings lightly rising from every small trifle and quarrels usually picked he was chased out of her presence" are an exact summary of Goneril's methods with her father[3]:

> GON. Put on what weary negligence you please,
> You and your fellows; I'ld have it come to question:
> * * * * * *
> And let his knights have colder looks among you;
> What grows of it, no matter; advise your fellows so:
> I would breed from hence occasions, and I shall.

---

[1] I. iv.   [2] II. iv.   [3] I. iii.

Darnley's heart, we are told, was "obstinately fixed" in loving Mary, and Lear is terribly hard to disenchant with Goneril and harder still to disenchant with Regan[1]:

> 'Tis not in thee
> To grudge my pleasures, to cut off my train;
> To bandy hasty words.

All this is self-deception but Lear, like Darnley, will insist on trying to trust where no trust is possible; Lear, like Darnley, is excluded with "dishonourable disdain" and like Darnley is shut out "in solitary desert to bewail his woeful miseries."

No parallels could be closer.

We may quote another most striking passage from Buchanan:

> When the king heard thereof (i.e. of the queen's sickness) he posted in haste to Jedwith....So far was it from his lodging and things necessary were provided against his coming (which is wont to be done even for mean persons) that he found not any token towards him of a friendly mind.
>
> But this was a point of most barbarous inhumanity used against him, that the nobility and all the officers of the Court that were present were specially forbidden, not once to do him reverence at his coming, not to yield him their lodging nor to harbour him so much as one night.
>
> And whereas the Queen suspected that the Earl of Murray would show him courtesy, she practised with his wife to go home in haste and fain herself sick, and keep her bed, that at least by this colour, under pretence of her sickness, the king might be shut out of doors.
>
> Being thus denied all duties of civil kindness, the next day, with great grief of heart, he retired to his old solitary corner. In the meantime, while the king in that want of all things, and forsaken of all friends, scant with begging findeth room in a cottage, Bothwell...as it were in triumph over the king, was gloriously removed in sight of the people into the Queen's own lodging.

[1] II. iv.

Here again we have the exact situation shown to us in
King Lear and not shown in *any* of Shakespeare's literary
sources.

The main thing to observe is that Mary is not satisfied
with excluding Darnley herself; she knows that the Earl of
Murray would be likely to receive him so she practises with
Murray's wife to have him shut out of doors. This is precisely what happens to Lear; Goneril is not satisfied with
excluding him herself; she takes care to "practise" with
Regan so that Regan may also exclude him[1].

> GON.   I know his heart.
> What he hath utter'd I have writ my sister:
> If she sustain him and his hundred knights,
> When I have show'd the unfitness,—
>   *   *   *   *   *   *
> Inform her full of my particular fear;
> And thereto add such reasons of your own
> As may compact it more.

Before Darnley arrives the nobility and officers of the
Court had been specially forbidden to do him any reverence
or to yield him any lodging or "to harbour him so much
as one night." This is precisely what happens to Lear when
he goes to Regan. All has been prepared in order that he
may be rejected and turned away and not even a night's
hospitality permitted.

Buchanan, we have seen, employs the very phrase "shut
out of doors" with regard to Darnley and this is quite literally
what happens to Lear[2]:

> No, I will weep no more.—In such a night
> To shut me out!

so Gloucester says:

> Go in with me: my duty cannot suffer
> To obey in all your daughters' hard commands:

----

[1] I. iv.   [2] III. iv.

Though their injunction be to bar my doors,
And let this tyrannous night take hold upon you,
Yet have I ventur'd to come seek you out,
And bring you where both fire and food is ready.

It is notable that Gloucester has received the most definite instructions not to succour Lear just like the instructions which Buchanan says that Mary gave to her nobles. Now nothing like this refusal of ordinary fire, lodging and shelter occurs in any of the sources; but it certainly occurs in *King Lear* and in the history.

Buchanan says that Darnley "scant with begging findeth room in a cottage," and it was in a hovel on the heath, in straw, that Lear ultimately found shelter.

Buchanan continues:

Her lawful husband, at the christening of his own child, not only wanted all maintenance for his necessary expenses, but also was commanded not once to come in the ambassador's sight, his ordinary servants were removed from him, the nobility were enjoined not once to attend on him, nor to do him honour, nor in a manner to know him; the foreign ambassadors were warned not to talk with him, when yet the most part of the day they were all in the same castle where he was.

Once again we have exact parallels to Shakespeare's drama which also are not found in the literary sources. Mary was not satisfied with shutting out her husband and removing his servants, even the nobility and ambassadors are warned to have no conference with him.

This, again, is precisely what happens to Lear. Goneril removes his servants, she prevents Regan from receiving him and she is still not satisfied but must command Gloucester to have nothing to do with him[1].

Alack, alack, Edmund, I like not this unnatural dealing. When I desired their leave that I might pity him, they took from me

[1] III. iii.

the use of mine own house; charged me, on pain of their perpetual displeasure, neither to speak of him, entreat for him, nor any way sustain him.

Gloucester continues:

Go to; say you nothing. There's a division betwixt the dukes ...these injuries the king now bears will be revenged home; there's part of a power already footed: we must incline to the king.

This again precisely represents the situation in Scotland where quarrels arose between the factious nobles and where there was always a party ready for their own sakes to support Darnley which was precisely what made Darnley formidable.

Buchanan continues:

The young gentleman thus contemptuously and unkindly used fell in such despair, that he departed from Sterling. At his departure the Queen still pursued him with her wonted hatred. All his silver plate wherewith he was served from his marriage until that day, she took it away every whit, and appointed pewter in the stead thereof.

...the rest that followed are evident arguments of outrageous cruelty and unappeasable hatred.

I have called attention before to the fact that in *King Lear* the hatred Goneril and Regan feel for their father is causeless and inexplicable, they have no reason whatever for their persecution which, also, is unutterably mean; they will not allow him to have " ten servants, nor five, nor one."

Buchanan proceeds:

Bothwell provided all things ready that were needed to accomplish the heinous act, first of all a house not commodious for a rich man, nor comely for a king, for it was both torn and ruinous, and had stood empty without any dweller for diverse years before; in a place of small resort, between the old fallen walls of two kirks, near a few almshouses for poor beggars.

Once again we have close parallels with *King Lear*.

It is in just such a place that Lear finds refuge; the house is "torn and ruinous" and standing empty; it also is in a place of small resort; Darnley's refuge is near a few almshouses for poor beggars and Edgar comes to Lear's hovel disguised as a beggar.

The author of the *Oration* follows exactly the same lines:

> If they demand the cause of so heinous a deed, I answer that it was unappeasable hatred. I demand of them again if they can deny that such hatred was, or that the same hatred was so great as without blood could not be satisfied. If they deny that such hatred was then let them answer me why she, a young woman, rich, noble and finally a queen, thrust away from her in manner into exile, the young gentleman...entirely loving her, in depth of sharp winter, into places neither fruitful of things necessary, nor replenished with inhabitants, and commonly perilous with haunt of thieves, why sent she him away into desert and barren craggy mountains, without provision, into open perils and in manner without any company....
>
> What else could she have done if she most deadly hated him....

Here again is a passage which gives us the central situation of *King Lear*.

There is the intense and violent and unprovoked hatred which Shakespeare, quite contrary to the old *Chronicle* tale, makes one of the main motives of his play. There is, once again, the "thrusting away into exile" of the man "entirely loving her." The inclemency of the weather is dwelt upon; the "depth of sharp winter" is as bad as Shakespeare's tempest which also, we may observe, was intensely cold.

Darnley is thrust away into places not "replenished with inhabitants" and Lear's heath was certainly such a place.

Darnley is thrust away into places "perilous with haunt. of thieves" and Lear has no companion but the madman and beggar—Edgar. Darnley is thrust away "into desert and barren craggy mountains," "in manner without any company." So is Lear thrust out on his heath, so has he no company but the fool and the beggar madman.

Could it be possible to give more accurately the central situation of Shakespeare's drama? And there is not a hint of it in the *Chronicles*.

The *Oration* draws a contrast between Mary "rich, noble and finally a queen" and the abject poverty into which she excludes Darnley, and Lear draws a similar heart-rending contrast between Regan and his own exclusion[1]:

> thou art a lady;
> If only to go warm were gorgeous,
> Why, nature needs not what thou gorgeous wear'st,
> Which scarcely keeps thee warm.

The *Oration* continues:

Call to mind that part of her letters to Bothwell wherein she maketh herself Medea, that is a woman that neither in love nor in hatred can keep any mean...she hated and not meanly hated him.

The *Oration* compares Mary to Medea and surely there is no figure in modern literature so like Medea as the dreadful figure of Goneril: the woman who betrays and ill-treats her father, who has no shame in her love, who poisons her sister and who also is betrayed with cold callousness by the object of her shameless passion.

The *Oration* continues to speak of Darnley's exclusion after the birth of his child:

What else shall one say she meant thereby, but as the poet sayth for pure love God wot she shut him out of doors. But this tender creature either shutteth out her husband, or as soon as he is come chaceth him away again, whose stomach

[1] II. iv.

turns at the sight of him and who is suddenly taken with pangs at his presence.

Here again we have the ironic contrast, so marked in *King Lear*, between the professions of love and the "shutting out of doors"; here we have the statement applied to Darnley, "she chaceth him away again," which is certainly exactly what happens to Lear with Regan.

The *Oration* proceeds to enumerate all the occasions on which Darnley was turned away to make room for the adulterer and says: "I am content to believe she did it not for hatred to her husband but for fancy's sake," but

> That she gave special commandment that no man should lodge him, that no man should relieve him with meat or drink, that she in a manner forbade him the use of fire and water, this is undoubtedly token of outrageous hatred.

It is always, we see, the same central situation. Darnley is repeatedly and cruelly excluded, shut out by the being on whom he has most claim; so also is Lear repeatedly excluded by a furious and causeless hate. As for the command: "that no man should relieve him with meat, or drink, that no man should lodge him," we have already seen that Gloucester had received exactly the same instructions with regard to Lear[1].

Kent implores Gloucester:

> Importune him once more to go, my lord;
> His wits begin to unsettle,

and Gloucester answers:

> Canst thou blame him?
> His daughters seek his death.

Just as Darnley's death was deliberately sought for, so

---

[1] III. iv.

we have Gloucester's word that Lear's death was deliberately sought for[1]:

> I have o'er-heard a plot of death upon him:
> *   *   *   *   *   *
> If thou shouldst dally half an hour, his life,
> With thine, and all that offer to defend him,
> Stand in assurèd loss.

The plot here is surely as grave as the plot against
Darnley. As for the refusal of the "use of fire and water,"
we may compare what Cordelia says[2]:

> Mine enemy's dog,
> Though he had bit me, should have stood that night
> Against my fire.

The *Oration* continues:

That she sent him back from Craigmillar to Sterling I com-
plain not. But that she bereaved him of all his necessaries, that
she took from him his servants,...that she alienated the nobility
from him...and (as much as in her lay) took from him even
while he lived the use of heaven, earth and air; this, I say, I
doubt what to call it, unnaturalness, hatred, barbarous fierceness or outrageous cruelty...the poor king lived in desolation,
in sorrow and beggary.

It is always the same situation which is the central situation in *King Lear*, the taking away of the servants is the
only part which resembles the old *Chronicle* story; all the
rest of Shakespeare's play resembles the history only. We
have the deliberate alienation of the nobility as Goneril
attempts to alienate Gloucester; the taking away from him,
even while he lived, of the "use of heaven, earth and air,"
which is startlingly applicable to Lear, banished to a heath
and crowded into a wretched hovel with only musty straw
to lie in.

[1] III. vi.   [2] IV. vii.

Kent implores him to enter the hovel[1]:

> Repose you there; while I to this hard house
> (More harder than the stones whereof 'tis rais'd,
> Which even but now, demanding after you,
> Denied me to come in) return and force
> Their scanted courtesy,

and Lear replies:

> Where is this straw, my fellow?
> The art of our necessities is strange,
> That can make vile things precious. Come, your hovel.

The intense coldness of the night on which Lear is shut out is dwelt upon exactly as Buchanan dwells on the coldness of the winter. Edgar cries [2]:

> Through the sharp hawthorn blows the wind,
> Hum! go to thy cold bed, and warm thee.

The *Oration* continues:

> But how great and unappeasable this hatred was, even by this ye may gather. Her husband so oft shut out...driven to extreme poverty, banished into a desolate corner...far from presence of men, spoiled of his servants and furniture of household,...yet by no injuries can be shaken from her, by no fear of death can be withdrawn but...he assayeth, if not to overcome, at least to combat the violent cruelty of her unkind courage.

It is always the same reiteration as in Lear; always the being shut out and driven into a desolate corner, always the motive of the servants being taken away.

> Regan[3]:
> She hath abated me of half my train;
> Look'd black upon me; struck me with her tongue,
> Most serpent-like, upon the very heart:

---

[1] III. ii.   [2] III. iv.   [3] II. iv.

and again:

> Return to her, and fifty men dismiss'd?
> No, rather, I abjure all roofs, and choose
> To be a comrade with the wolf and owl.

and again:

> GON. What need you five and twenty, ten, or five,
> *   *   *   *   *
> REG.   What need one?

As for the absence of furniture we notice that one of Lear's refuges contains, apparently, only straw; the other seems to have nothing much beside joint-stools. Cordelia speaks of him as limited to "short and musty straw[1]."

The *Oration* proceeds:

> Neither is she once moved with the loving doings, nor with the wretched plight, nor with the miserable woefulness of her husband, nor appeased by time, nor satisfied by torments, but rather with his serviceableness she is irritated...at every time of his coming she deviseth some new increase of spiteful dishonour...he was despised of all men and thrown into open perils.

It is continually the same situation which is reiterated and it is the central situation in *King Lear*. It is said of Mary that, each time Darnley approaches her, she treats him with some "new increase of spiteful dishonour." Could there be a better description of the attitude Goneril and Regan take towards Lear? Their intense spitefulness combines with their insensate hatred to make them the most utterly loathsome women in Shakespeare.

The *Oration* continues:

> By this time I suppose you see the hatred of the queen...how unappeasable, how outrageously cruel, how obstinate it was against her husband, whom she thrust among thieves...whom

[1] IV. vii.

naked and poor, loaden with despites, vexed with railings, assailed with poison, she drove away into a solitary corner there to die with extremest torment.

Here we have again the metaphor of nakedness which is employed with such dreadful effect in *King Lear*[1].

LEAR. Why, thou wert better in thy grave, than to answer with thy uncovered body this extremity of the skies.—Is man no more than this?...Thou art the thing itself:...Off, off, you lendings!—Come, unbutton here.

It is possible that Murray gave Shakespeare hints for the character of Kent:

"Murray," says the *Oration*, "was also hated by the queen, her hatred was 'the cause that so often brought him in danger of death...that made him rather choose to go into banishment than to remain in court among ruffians'."

Murray was banished, we may observe, through Darnley's anger but returned privately and in concealment in the endeavour to help him to get the Crown matrimonial. So does Kent return from banishment to help Lear in the hope to deliver Lear and ultimately to return him to power[2].

Another point of resemblance lies in the desire Darnley has "to go beyond sea." Lear, when he is turned away by Regan, takes flight for Dover and it is on his way there that he is re-captured. Now this also has a parallel in the history. De Croc wrote October 15th, 1566:

The Queen is now returned from Stirling to Edinburgh. The King, however, abode at Stirling, and he told me there that he had a mind to go beyond sea in a sort of desperation.... The Bishop of Ross by the Queen's commandment declared to the Council the King's intention to go beyond sea, for which purpose he had a ship lying ready to sail....Therefore the Queen prayed the King to declare in presence of the Lords and before me the reason of his projected departure....I likewise took the

[1] III. iv.   [2] III. i.

freedom to tell him that his departure must certainly affect either his own or the Queen's honour....The King...went out of the chamber of presence saying: "Adieu, Madam, you shall not see my face for a long space."

On May 7th, 1566, Drury wrote to Cecil[1]: "The misliking between the Queen and her husband increases so that it is judged he cannot in safety dwell long in Scotland," and again on May 23rd: "It goes yet very hardly between the noblemen and the Queen of Scots, but specially with her husband who goes into Flanders."

This again corresponds very closely with the situation in *King Lear* where Gloucester is certain that the death of Lear is determined and wishes to hurry him to Dover to get him out of the country or to meet Cordelia's force. He has to answer why he wished to convey the king to Dover and he answered truthfully because he did not wish to see Regan:

In his anointed flesh stick boarish fangs[2].

---

[1] *State Papers*, Foreign Series.   [2] III. vii.

CHAPTER XII

BOTHWELL AND EDMUND—
RIZZIO AND OSWALD

In the previous chapter I have several times alluded to
what I believe to be a connection between the character of
Bothwell and the story of Edmund. The story of Edmund's
callous love-making to the two sisters conjointly, his de-
ception of both and their furious jealousy of each other
offers the closest resemblances to the Mary and Darnley
story as shown in the *Casket Letters* and as told by Buchanan.
We may remember, also, that this portion of *King Lear* is
entirely Shakespeare's own introduction; he certainly did
not find it in the story of Lear and neither did he find it in
Sidney's *Arcadia*, for the tale of the blind king of Paphlagonia contains no love-story—it concerns solely the relation
of the father to the two sons.

The *Casket Letters* which were certainly believed by the
Protestants of the time to be genuine and which were, of
course, available as a source for Shakespeare, show Mary's
bitter resentment at being tied to Darnley and her anger
and jealousy against Bothwell's wife. Letter I says:

Cursed may this pockish man be, that causes me have so
much pain, for without him I would have a far more pleasant
subject to discourse upon.

Letter II reads:

You have never heard him speak better nor more humbly;
and if I had not proof of his heart to be as waxe, and that
mine were not as a diamond, no stroke but coming from your
hand would make me but to have pity on him. But fear not

for the place shall continue till death. Remember also, in re-
compense thereof, not to suffer yours to be won by that false
race that would do no less to yourself.

...He has always the tears in his eye. He saluteth every
man, even to the meanest, and maketh much of them that
they may take pity of him.

...See not also her feigned tears; you ought not more to
regard them than the true travails which I endure to deserve
her place, for obtaining of which against my own nature, I
do betray those that would let me.

We may notice, incidentally, how closely this passage resembles Lear. When Mary says of Darnley that he salutes
every man, even to the meanest, and makes much of them
that they may pity him, we are surely reminded of Lear
and his wretchedness when he seeks sympathy even from
the beggar Edmund and the fool.

In his anguish he expresses a deep compassion for the
poor[1]:

> Poor naked wretches, wheresoe'er you are,
> That bide the pelting of this pitiless storm,
> How shall your houseless heads, and unfed sides,
> Your loop'd and window'd raggedness, defend you
> From seasons such as these?

The main situation, surely, is exactly like that of Goneril,
resenting keenly her tie to Albany and furiously jealous of
her sister Regan.

Goneril speaks as contemptuously of Albany as Mary
does of Darnley[2]:

> It is the cowish terror of his spirit,
> That dares not undertake: he'll not feel wrongs
> Which tie him to an answer.
>   *   *   *   *   *   *
> Decline your head; this kiss, if it durst speak,
> Would stretch thy spirits up into the air:
> Conceive, and fare thee well,

[1] III. iv.   [2] IV. ii.

and again:

> O, the difference of man and man!
> To thee a woman's services are due:
> My fool usurps my body.

So soon afterwards, in exactly the same way as Mary scorns Darnley, does Goneril heap her contempt on Albany (who bears, be it remembered, the same historical title, for Darnley was actually Duke of Albany).

Similar also is Goneril's jealousy of her sister especially when Regan, after Cornwall's death, becomes available as a legal wife.

> I had rather lose the battle, than that sister
> Should loosen him and me[1],

and we have also Edmund's reflections on the situation[2]:

> To both these sisters have I sworn my love;
> Each jealous of the other, as the stung
> Are of the adder. Which of them shall I take?
> Both? one? or neither?

This exactly represents the situation as depicted in the *Casket Letters* and in Mary's appended sonnets.

Even the love-letters of Regan[3]:

> Therefore I do advise you, take this note:
> My lord is dead; Edmund and I have talk'd;
> And more convenient is he for my hand
> Than for your lady's:...
> If you do find him, pray you, give him this.

Even these love-letters have their parallel in the curious sonnets Mary and Lady Bothwell wrote to Bothwell in rivalry:

> Elle pour son honneur vous doibt obeyssance,
> Moy vous obeyssant c'en puis recevoir blasme,
> N'estât, à mon regret, comme elle vostre femme.
> Et si n'aura pourtant en ce point pre-eminence
> Pour son propre profit.

---

[1] v. i.　　　　　[2] v. i.　　　　　[3] IV. v.

184 Bothwell and Edmund—Rizzio and Oswald

In Sonnet 6, an extraordinary production, Mary accuses her rival of borrowing her love-letters and love-poems from literary sources and declares that Lady Bothwell expresses her love for her husband in phrases which are not hers :

> Et toutesfois ses parolles fardeez
> Ses pleurs, ses plaincts remplis de fictions.
> Et ses hautz cris et lamentations
> Ont tant gaigné que par vous sont gardéez
> Ses lettres aux quelles vous donnez foy
> Et si l'aymez et croyez plus que moy.

Sonnet 9 is an impassioned expression of the way in which for Bothwell's sake Mary has given up her honour, yielded up her greatness and conscience and left her relatives and friends:

> Pour luy depuis jay mesprise l'honneur
> Ce qui nous peult seul pouvoir de bonheur.
> Pour luy hazarde grandeur et conscience.
> Pour luy…j'ay quité parentz et amis,
> Et tous autres respectz sont apart mis.

Here again we have an exact counterpart to the recklessness and dishonour of Goneril; it is equally true that she scorns her honour for the sake of Edmund, that she risks her greatness for his sake; it is for Edmund that Goneril has lost husband and friends and tramples on "all other respects." We may note as a further parallel that, when Goneril is finally ruined, it is by means of the love-letters that she has written to Edmund and that she tries to assert that the law is hers and what she chooses to make of it. Here again the parallel is precise for Mary was ruined mainly by the so-called *Casket Letters*, the love-letters to Bothwell from which we have been quoting, and she certainly believed that she was above the law.

ALB.   Shut your mouth, dame,
Or with this paper shall I stop it:—hold, sir;
Thou worse than any name, read thine own evil:—
No tearing, lady; I perceive you know it.
                    (*Gives the letter to* EDMUND.)
GON. Say, if I do,—the laws are mine, not thine:
Who can arraign me for't?
ALB.   Most monstrous! oh!
Know'st thou this paper?
GON.   Ask me not what I know.

Here we have Goneril confronted and ruined by her own
love-letters to Edmund, just as Mary was confronted and
ruined by her love-letters to Bothwell.

It is obvious, also, that Goneril has planned her husband's
death for she has, at any rate, definitely arranged her
marriage with Edmund.

Albany says:

For your claim, fair sister,
I bar it in the interest of my wife;
'Tis she is sub-contracted to this lord,
And I, her husband, contradict your bans.
If you will marry, make your loves to me,
My lady is bespoke[1].

The curious detail of the rival love-letters between the
two sisters is exactly paralleled in Sonnet 6.

Buchanan in his *Detection* speaks with bitter anger of the
contract for Mary's marriage having been made before
Bothwell's divorce. He says:

This contract was made the 5th of April, within eight weeks
after the murder of the King...also it was made seven days
before Bothwell was acquitted, by corrupt judgment, of the
said murder. Also it appears by the words of the contract
itself, that it was made before sentence of divorce between
Bothwell and his former wife, and also in very truth was made
before any suit of divorce intended or begun between him and
his former wife.

[1] v. iii.

Here again we may note the close parallel in the situation: Edmund claimed by Goneril at the very moment when Regan claims him on a pre-contract:

> Reg.   In my rights,
>   By me invested, he compeers the best.
> Gon. That were the most, if he should husband you.
> Reg. Jesters do oft prove prophets[1].

Moreover Lady Bothwell was, apparently, as jealous of Mary as Regan of Goneril; thus on April 30th, 1567 Drury wrote to Cecil:

> The Lady Bothwell is now for the yielding to the divorce of another mind, and says she will never say untruly of herself, but will die with the name of the Lady Bothwell[2].

We may compare Regan:

>   Now, sweet lord,
>   You know the goodness I intend upon you;
>   Tell me,—but truly,—but then speak the truth,
>   Do you not love my sister?
>   *   *   *   *   *
>   I never shall endure her: dear my lord,
>   Be not familiar with her[3].

Even after the marriage the rivalry did not cease for Mary remained furiously jealous of Bothwell's former wife. Thus on June 21st, 1567 de Silva writes[4]:

> They say for certain that differences have arisen already between Bothwell and the Queen (an evil conscience can know no peace) and it is asserted that Bothwell passes some days a week with the wife he had divorced.

Bothwell, of course, commanded as large forces in Scotland as Edmund commands in *King Lear*. Thus we find Kirkaldy of Grange writing to Bedford on May 8th, 1567:

> The chief occasion why these noblemen desire the Queen of England's aid is rather to take Bothwell out of Dunbar and

---

[1] v. iii.   [2] *State Papers*, Foreign Series.
[3] v. i.   [4] Simancas Papers.

Edinburgh; not only has he the two principal strengths, but also all the munition of the realm.

This exactly resembles the situation in *King Lear* where Regan gives all her armies into Edmund's charge even while she remains savagely jealous of her sister.

> REG. Methinks our pleasure might have been demanded,
> Ere you had spoke so far. He led our powers;
> Bore the commission of my place and person;
>   *   *   *   *   *   *
> GON.   Not so hot:
> In his own grace he doth exalt himself,
> More than in your addition.
> REG.   In my rights,
> By me invested, he compeers the best[1].

It is also curiously interesting to observe that these historical events were put into dramas at the time. Thus, Drury writes to Cecil, May 14th, 1567:

> There has been an interlude of boys at Stirling of the manner of the king's death and the arraignment of the earl....This was before the Lords, who the Earl thinks were devisers of the same.

Even the poisoning of Regan had its prototype in the Darnley story. It is true that Lady Bothwell was not poisoned but it was very generally believed at the time that such an attempt had been made. Thus de Silva, the Spanish Ambassador, asserted that there was a plan for Bothwell to get rid of his wife either by divorce or by poison. On March 30th, 1567 we find Giovanni Correr in France writing concerning Scottish affairs:

> The Cardinal of Lorraine has been warned by letters from his friends in Scotland that many of the chief personages there had suspicion, and had almost come to the conclusion that he had advised and procured the death of the king, and that he must therefore be upon his guard.

[1] v. iii.

...In confirmation of the above the English ambassador gives out...that almost immediately after the death of the King of Scotland the wife of one of the principal personages of the kingdom died of poison and it was reported that a marriage between the queen and this personage would follow.

This extract is doubly interesting because it shows how commonly the Darnley murder was believed to have been one of the crimes of the House of Lorraine and how many people believed that the poisoning of Bothwell's wife had really taken effect.

We may compare the situation in *King Lear*:

> REG.   Sick, O sick!
> GON. (*Aside*) If not, I'll ne'er trust medicine.
>   *   *   *   *   *
> REG. My sickness grows upon me.

Later on we hear that Regan is dead and that Goneril has confessed to poisoning her:

> GENT. Your lady, sir, your lady; and her sister
>   By her is poison'd; she hath confess'd it,

and Edmund replies:

> I was contracted to them both.

Here again it seems to me impossible to overlook the parallel situation. When we remember that this love-story was in neither of Shakespeare's sources and that it exists quite clear and definite in the history, we must surely confess that the historical source is far and away closer to Shakespeare's drama than any possible combination of the accepted literary sources.

The character of Oswald, again, is not to be found in any of the *Chronicles*, either in Geoffrey of Monmouth or in Hclinshed. On the other hand Rizzio as a servant, Rizzio as an impudent, low-born mischief-maker repeatedly appears as a source of discord between Mary and Darnley.

On February 7th, 1566, Randolph writes to Cecil:

David yet retaineth still his place not without heart-grief to many that see their sovereign guided chiefly by such a fellow.

David Chalmer's *Chronicle* (1572) says:

There was a servant of the Queen's who was an Italian, called David Riccio...who was but a man of base lineage....This David came in great favour with her Majesty, but greatly misliked of all the people, yet she made him her servitor and secretary.

...he showed all the malice he could to sow discord between the Earl Murray and the Lord Darnley, thinking thereby to get the Earl of Murray out of Court, whom he esteemed then his greatest unfriend and so it came to pass that the Earl was constrained to leave Court.

...David dealt with the nobility that the Lords should be forfalted, which procured the malice of the whole people to him.

Melville says in his *Memoirs*:

David Rizzio was retained in her service as a varlet of her chamber...he grew so great that he presented all signatures to be subscribed by her Majesty; that some of the nobility would gloom upon him, and some of them would shoulder him and shoot him by, when they entered in the Chamber and found him always speaking with her Majesty.

Now here we have again a situation almost exactly similar to that in *King Lear*.

Rizzio is a main cause of the difficulties between Mary and Darnley, and Oswald is made a main cause of the difficulties between Lear and Goneril and is certainly the agent of Goneril's meanest cruelties; he is a servant, a "varlet," a man of low birth, yet he is particularly insolent; he makes it his business to insult Lear. I have pointed out before the parallel between Murray and Kent and here again we notice that, just as Rizzio came into special conflict with Murray and was the cause of his being banished from the Court, so Oswald came into special conflict with Kent.

Lear despises Oswald just as furiously as Darnley despised Rizzio.

He asks concerning him[1]: "Where's that mongrel?" and in the next sentence "Why came not the slave back to me when I called him?"

It is Oswald who taunts Lear with his powerlessness and with being no more than "My lady's father" and in the end provokes Lear to strike him.

Oswald, we observe, is Goneril's secretary, for it is he who writes to Regan on her behalf:

> How now, Oswald.
> What, have you writ that letter to my sister?

In Kent's quarrel with Oswald we have exactly such a character ascribed to the latter as the friends of Darnley ascribed to Rizzio[2]:

> A knave; a rascal; an eater of broken meats; a base, proud, shallow, beggarly, three-suited, hundred-pound, filthy, worsted-stocking knave; a lily-liver'd, action-taking knave; a whoreson glass-gazing, super-serviceable, finical rogue; one-trunk-inheriting slave....Draw, you rascal: you come with letters against the king,

and when Cornwall asks Kent "Why art thou angry?" Kent replies:

> That such a slave as this should wear a sword,
> That wears no honesty. Such smiling rogues as these,
> Like rats, oft bite the holy cords a-twain
> Which are too intrinse t' unloose;...
> A plague upon your epileptic visage!

Now this was exactly the view of Rizzio's character taken by the Scottish Lords; it is not one whit too strong and it is certainly the view taken of Rizzio's function in the state.

We observe also the parallel in point of time. When

---

[1] I. iv.   [2] II. ii.

Goneril first starts the persecution of Lear, Oswald is her instrument; it is this base servant and secretary who deliberately insults the powerless king, who incites him and his followers to frenzy, and it is a quarrel concerning Oswald which brings about the final rupture between Lear and Goneril.

So, when Mary first quarrelled with Darnley, it was Mary's confidence in Rizzio that enraged him; it was the precedence of a man so base-born which drove the proud Stuart to frenzy; he was filled with hatred and contempt for the "varlet" and it was, of course, the Rizzio murder which brought about the final rupture with Mary.

In the second part of the play Oswald passes out of sight but Goneril was at that time absorbed with her paramour—Edmund—and her rivalry with Regan; it is Edmund who is made the instrument for the final destruction of Lear. So again, when the Rizzio trouble was at an end between Mary and her husband it was only to give way to the still more serious Bothwell trouble and to Mary's infatuation for a man who was, just as Edmund was to Goneril, her leading soldier and also her leading noble.

CHAPTER XIII

KING LEAR AND ST BARTHOLOMEW

I POINTED out in dealing with *Macbeth* that the Gunpowder
Plot had reminded the English of the massacre of St Bartholomew and that material chosen from the story of the
Coligny murder appeared to have been used in the com-
pilation of *Macbeth*.

This also I believe to be, but in an even more interesting
manner, the case with *King Lear*.

Let us remember that, before the Gunpowder Plot reminded England of these two crimes, they had already been
associated in the popular mind. Thus in the Huguenot
Memoirs[1] I have so often quoted, the St Bartholomew
massacre and the Darnley murder are treated as parallel
crimes, both inspired by the Catholic League, both planned
and executed by the House of Lorraine and Catherine de
Médici, and in each case there was supposed to have been
direct contact with the powers of hell. Agrippa d'Aubigné
accuses Catherine of witch-practices precisely similar to
those already analysed in *Macbeth*[2].

Buchanan's account of the Darnley murder, the very
account we have been studying in the preceding chapters,
is inserted into the midst of a narrative of the affairs of
France.

The Darnley murder was repeatedly termed a "parricide" by contemporaries and exactly the same term was
applied to the Coligny murder. The royal family of France,

[1] *Memoires de l'estat de France sous Charles IX.*
[2] *Les Tragiques.*

Catherine, Margaret and Charles IX, were in the habit of addressing Coligny as "father." Very naturally this title lent a horrible irony to the circumstances of his murder. The Huguenots, in their intense admiration for Coligny, termed him the "father" of his country and compared France to an ungrateful child destroying its father.

Then, again, Coligny possessed almost regal power. The house from which he descended had certain royal privileges, among them being the right to have a personal retinue of a hundred knights. Moreover Coligny's power over a certain portion of France, particularly the provinces of the Loire, was so absolute that he was practically a king in that region; he was very generally known as "the second king of France." I might mention here that the river Loire (the Liger of the Romans) is known as the river of Lear in such Elizabethan chronicles as Fabyan, so the provinces of the Loire would be to an Elizabethan the provinces of Lear. Spenser terms Coligny Guyon[1] (i.e. Guienne) and the name of Lear points just as plainly to the region of his power[2].

It was, of course, jealousy of Coligny's almost royal power which urged on Catherine de Médici to her dreadful deed. It was the same idea which caused the Parisian populace to crown the effigy of Coligny with straw. Shakespeare's Lear, we may remark, crowns himself with wild flowers which are flowers of the field.

Coligny was also considered as being in quite a special way, the victim of his own over-confidence and the prey of his own excessive trust. Many members of his own party, including the ever-faithful Joan of Navarre, had warned him against Charles IX and Catherine, but Coligny believed

---

[1] *Faerie Queene*, Bk. II.
[2] NOTE. He was also Grand Admiral of France and, as such, would have control over the Ligurian Sea which is known as the Sea of Lear.

in the professions of affection made to him by the royal family; he trusted himself completely in their power, the result being one of the most infamous betrayals in history.

Coligny seemed to his friends at the time as if he were almost besotted with excess of confidence.

Now in certain of its main outlines the Coligny story really does resemble the Darnley story; in both we have flattery and false professions of affection used to ensnare a victim, in both cases the murder is termed a "parricide." In both cases the victim has possessed either royal power or a claim to royal power.

It was thus not difficult for Shakespeare to blend the two stories in one and here, exactly as in *Macbeth*, he was working to a pre-existent unity in the minds of his audience. The supreme pathos of Lear, his helplessness, his futile rages are derived from the story of Darnley, which even modern historians have termed "the most pathetic in the annals of Scotland." But there is more in Shakespeare's Lear than pathos; there is a terrific force and energy, there is a Titanic power and passion, heroic courage and heroic dignity which cannot have been derived from the Darnley story alone, but which are entirely appropriate to Coligny and still more appropriate if Coligny is taken as representative of France itself.

Neither does Bothwell's invention of the thunderstorm seem in the least adequate to suggest the terrific thunderstorm in *King Lear* which is surely one of the most appalling tempests ever conceived by the imagination of man. On the other hand the civil wars in France are repeatedly compared to a terrific tempest sweeping the land, filled with lightnings of wrath and hate, drowning France in deluges of her own tears, filled with cyclones of lamentations and bitterly cold, cold with the absence of all human charity[1].

---

[1] See *Memoires sur l'estat de France sous Charles IX*, also P. Mathieu's *Deplorable Death of Henry IV*, also D'Aubigné's *Les Tragiques*.

It was simply the commonest of all metaphors for the Civil Wars. Now surely a conception like this is great enough even for the tempest in *King Lear*?

Now Shakespeare's Lear is depicted as an old man but still a man of tremendous force and energy; Coligny, at the time he was murdered, was an old man as that time counted age and he himself appealed to his murderers to respect his white hairs, yet Coligny was a man still of tremendous physical force; the Lear of Shakespeare had been a great soldier, accustomed to war, so had Coligny who was undoubtedly one of the greatest soldiers of his age.

The Lear of Shakespeare is a man of terrific passions, capable of most appalling rages and unequalled imprecations; so was Coligny who, when angry, rated the whole royal family of France with the utmost fury.

Lear is stripped naked in a tempest and deserted of all; we have already recalled the terrible story of how the naked body of Coligny, deserted by all, was exposed to the jeers of the passers-by. The body was thrown into the Seine, dragged out again, hanged on a gallows and a fire was lit beneath; Coligny's followers said that his naked body was exposed to all the outrages of the elements of fire, earth, air and water. So is Lear's naked body exposed to the outrages of the elements. Coligny's followers dèclared that Coligny was the father of his country, outraged by his ungrateful children and that all France suffered in his person. All France is with him exposed naked to the tempest of St Bartholomew. Singing ribald songs the populace of Paris crowned the effigy of Coligny with straw, and, singing senseless songs, Lear crowns himself with wild flowers.

After his death Coligny's very furniture was judged and condemned to be destroyed, and in *King Lear* we have the bitter irony of the trial of the joint-stools.

13—2

Here, surely, we have ideas tremendous enough even for Shakespeare's drama? If we regard Lear as being simply the story of a remote king in the bronze age whose tale, in the original, was *not a tragedy at all*, then surely it is much too appallingly great for its subject?

But if Lear is, in some sort at least, the tragedy of a whole nation agonizing in the horrors of civil war, the tragedy of one of the greatest nations of the world reduced almost to the level of the brutes, when we remember that Shakespeare probably feared a similar fate for his own country, then the reason for his terrific grief becomes at once manifest.

Read Agrippa d'Aubigné's *Les Tragiques*[1], his lamentations over the fathers who try to murder their sons, the sons who drive their fathers into exile, the brothers who fight in a duel to the death, the old men groping with trembling hands over the bodies of their children dead before them, the deluges of tears, the lightnings, the bitter cold, the food which is rats and mice and even human dung—study all this and you will see for yourself either that *Les Tragiques* contains D'Aubigné's reminiscences of *King Lear*, or at least that he is describing precisely similar things.

Nor is D'Aubigné the only French author who shows this close resemblance.

As we have said, P. Mathieu, the Historiographer-Royal of France, tells us how France was like a father who preferred an illegitimate son—Henry, Duke of Guise—to the legitimate son—Henry of Navarre; how the legitimate son was banished and reduced to the most miserable poverty; how the illegitimate son triumphed but betrayed his father into enemy hands (i.e. those of Spain); he tells how Navarre, even in poverty and disgrace, remained loyal to his father-

---

[1] Commenced 1577, published 1616.

land—France—and guided and helped it; how when his fatherland, mutilated and its eyes closed, was about to dash itself to pieces, he—Navarre—intervened and saved it[1].

In *King Lear* the conflict between the two sons is ultimately decided by gage of battle and Edgar (still nominally an exile) wins back his right. This also corresponds to the history, for Navarre did, of course, ultimately win his kingdom by force of arms.

Let us deal now with the parallels in more detail:

On August 26th, 1566, Fitz-william writes to Cecil anent Coligny: "The admiral is of great power and well-beloved of all the best soldiers in France. It is thought that he has at commandment 30,000 men." Here we have the almost royal power of Coligny.

In the *Life of Jasper Colignie* by Golding, published by the Vautrollier Press in 1576, we read:

It is certain that that house had the right of sovereignty... they had power of life and death over the people of their signiory and to coin money...and to raise taxes.

Here we have both royal dignity and royal power.

Boulé[2] also says that Coligny was commonly known at the time as the "second king of France," that he was by temper dominant and haughty, violent in altercation and that, on one occasion, he offered the king ten thousand men as if he were himself a monarch:

Cependant, comme la reine mère croyait tout le parti consister dans la tête de Coligny, la mort de ce deuxième roi de France fut d'abord seule resolue....

Cependant l'amiral...était dur, hautain, mal habile, violentant les conseils, tenant des colloques secrets avec le roi. Il lui offrit un jour dix mille hommes.

Henry Martin says that Catherine urged on her son to

[1] *Deplorable Death of Henry IV*, Grimstone's translation, 1612.
[2] *Catherine de Médici and Coligny.*

the murder by telling him that the admiral played the part
of a king and treated him—Charles—as a subordinate;
"l'amiral joue le roi, fait de lui l'instrument de ses ambitions."

The Queen of Navarre was termed "sister" by the royal
family of France. Thus we read in a Huguenot tract published in 1573 at Basle and entitled: "Dialogues au quel
sont traites plusieurs choses avenues aux Lutheriens et
Huguenots de la France."

> La Royne de Navarre vint trouver à la fin le Roy duquel
> (ce disoit-il) elle estoit la meilleure tante, la plus desiree, la
> mieux aimee...la Royne-mere la recueillit comme sa tres chere
> sœur.

The same writer says the king treated Coligny "en son
pere propre."

We may also compare de Thou:

> Coligny came to Paris though the greatest number of his
> friends were opposed to it; they dissuaded him with impor-
> tunity both by speech and by letter. He, however, placed
> fullest confidence in the king. Some of the letters were very
> sharp; they reminded him that it was a decree of the Papists,
> confirmed by the Councils, that it was not necessary to keep
> faith with heretics.
>
> ...The king has been educated in a school in which he sucked
> in with his milk the lesson of making a game of oaths and of
> perjury and of taking in vain the name of God, and of de-
> faming himself by irreligion and dissimulation.
>
> ...He (Coligny) was advised to flee from the Court as from
> an infected cloaca.

De Thou adds "The King called Coligny 'father' because
of his age and merit."

Here we surely have a situation closely parallel with that
in *King Lear*. We have the misplaced confidence of the
victim who ignores the sharpest warnings given by his

friends; we have the enthusiastic professions of affection, the taking of false oaths in the name of God[1]:

> I love you more than words can wield the matter;
> Dearer than eye-sight, space, and liberty;

or

>   I profess
> Myself an enemy to all other joys,
> Which the most precious square of sense possesses;
> And find I am alone felicitate
> In your dear highness' love.

Remember that the death of Lear has already been de-cided and these words acquire a new irony and a new horror. The Huguenot *Memoires* sums up the situation: "L'Amiral convié à la Cour aux nopces d'une sœur de Roy, apres mille sermens et mille caresses, y est massacré." A thousand oaths and a thousand caresses really does express the attitude of Goneril and Regan to Lear, and if we know that, all the time, his murder was resolved we surely find a new depth of terror in Shakespeare's play?

Coligny was permitted a bodyguard of nobles when he came to the court, just as Lear, though renouncing all other powers, kept his bodyguard of knights. None the less Coligny's trust was so great that to his friends he appeared almost senseless. Laval[2] sums it up:

The admiral lulled by the great regard which the King feigned to have for him became almost senseless...he was angry with all those who were not so credulous as himself and could not bear to see distrust in anybody.

The Admiral, Laval insists, was repeatedly and con-tinuously warned but he could not believe: "he recalled to his mind the many repeated Oaths of the King, of his

---

[1] I. i.
[2] *History of the Reformation in France.*

Mother and of the Duke of Anjou and he would take no warning."

Now surely we have here a situation exactly paralleled in the opening scenes of *King Lear*; we have a venerable man termed "Father," the recipient of the deepest professions of affection confirmed by many oaths, who, as if besotted, accepts all these professions at their face value; we have him warned both by the lady who is called "sister" and by his faithful servants, we have his obstinate credulity and we have his anger against the very friends who warn him.

In order to make the parallel more precise we have the attitude assumed by the Queen of Navarre. She had no confidence in Catherine; she profoundly mistrusted the Court; she saw through all their flatteries and she could not understand Coligny's infatuation. We may quote from her last letter to her son:

> I am not at liberty to talk with the King, nor with Madam but only with the Queen Mother who deals with me very scurvily....
>
> I have complained three times to the Queen; but she laugh'd at me and behind my back makes me say quite the reverse of what I have said. In so much that I am blamed for it by my friends and I do not know how to give the lie to the Queen... she laughs in my face and uses me in such a manner that you may say that my patience exceeds Griselda's.
>
> ...I am sure if you knew the trouble I am in you would pity me; I am treated with the utmost rigour, vain talking and banters, instead of being treated with gravity....I have resolved not to put myself into a passion, it is a wonder to see my patience....The corruption is much greater than I could have imagined.

Here again we surely have the closest parallels to the opening scenes of *King Lear*. We have the figure of Joan of Navarre set over against Catherine and Margaret as

Cordelia is set over against Goneril and Regan. We have the impudent lies which Joan sees through but feels powerless to fight. We have Joan's perfect clearness of insight just as we have Cordelia's perfect clearness of insight:

> I know you what you are;
> And like a sister am most loath to call
> Your faults as they are named.

We have Joan's patience, comparing herself to Griselda, just as we have Cordelia's patience. We have Joan's contempt for the falsity of Catherine just as we have Cordelia's contempt for Goneril. Finally we must remember that Catherine calls Joan "sister."

Nearly all narratives of the Coligny murder begin with the story of the marriage. The *Memoires* already alluded to certainly does so and we notice that *King Lear* also begins with a marriage plan, for the marriage of Cordelia was to have been settled in the first scene; also the marriage involves the future disposal of the kingdom and the two are to be settled together; so did the actual historical marriage involve the future disposal of the kingdom.

The *Memoires* proceed to explain that part of the St Bartholomew plot was to withdraw Mary Queen of Scots from prison and make her Queen of England; this is a main reason why the Huguenots treat the two crimes—St Bartholomew and the Darnley murder—as one series of events destined to avert the Protestant succession in England and France, and to place both countries in the power of the Guises. This appears to have been the general Protestant point of view and it gives us an additional reason why the two crimes should be connected in the popular mind and why Shakespeare should link them together in a drama.

The *Memoires* give us first the French marriage and the flattery which entraps Coligny, then Buchanan's story of

Mary Queen of Scots and then the murder of Coligny; this is, very largely, Shakespeare's order in his play.

The *Memoires* narrate how Catherine de Médici murdered the Queen of Navarre; she was supposed to have been destroyed by poison, either by poisoned gloves or, in some versions, by a poisoned necklace. So in Shakespeare's play Cordelia is represented as murdered at the instigation of her sisters.

The *Memoires* dwells on the character of the Queen of Navarre; she uttered no word of complaint or impatience; she was wonderful in her constancy and firmness and truth. She was perfectly truthful though her enemies alienated even her husband and won him by flattery from her side.

Qui est un exemple rare et remarquable à la posterité; veu encore que depuis elle y a employé, je ne diray pas seulement jusques à ses bagues et joyaux, mais aussi hazardé sa vie mesme et tout ce que elle avoit de plus cher.

Her lands were declared forfeit and she herself dispossessed of all:

ne laissa-elle de porter le tout avec telle patience et magnanimité chretienne, qu'on ne pouvait dire qu'elle fit paroistre avoir aucun regret de s'etre embarqué en cette cause.

No remonstrances availed to make her change her religion and she possessed the most wonderful integrity; she never flattered or dissimulated: "elle n'espargnoit aucuns, ains rondement et sans rien flatter ou dissimuler."

Now surely this has the most wonderfully close resemblance to Cordelia? Cordelia also utters no word of complaint or impatience; like Joan of Navarre she is perfect in her dignity. Cordelia also is wonderful in firmness, constancy and truth; these are precisely the leading lines of her character as Shakespeare has drawn them. Just as Joan's nearest—her husband—was turned away from her and alienated by the wiles and flatteries of Catherine, so was Cordelia's best-beloved—Lear—alienated and turned away from her by the wiles of Goneril.

Just as Joan gave up all her possessions and lost her lands for the truth and ultimately life itself, so did Cordelia give up all her lands for the truth. Joan bore all this with patience and magnanimity; so did Cordelia bear it with patience and magnanimity.

No remonstrances or threats could make Joan change her religion, and no remonstrances and no threats could make Cordelia utter a word she believed untrue.

Joan has wonderful integrity and never flattered or dissimulated; so also has Cordelia wonderful integrity and it is her entire incapacity for flattery and dissimulation that does most to impassion us on her side.

It was in 1563 that the Pope published his celebrated Monitory against the Queen of Navarre; she was summoned to appear at Rome and in the event of her contumaciously refusing she was deprived of all her possessions and her kingdoms and principalities, sovereignties, lordships, domains—to be given to those on whom his Holiness may be pleased to bestow them.

St Croix made an offer to Antoine de Bourbon on behalf of the Pope that his marriage with Joan should be annulled, that she should be deprived of her dominions for the crime of heresy (as the Huguenots put it for the sake of "truth") and that these dominions should be bestowed on Antoine de Bourbon; his new bride was, of course, to be Mary Queen of Scots.

It seems to me that the parallel is complete. Cordelia also loses her inheritance because of her truthfulness; Lear repudiates her and is alienated from her and turns to Goneril.

CHAPTER XIV

KING LEAR AND ST BARTHOLOMEW (*cont.*)

COLIGNY was famous for the discipline he had introduced among his troops: Golding in his *Life of Jasper Colignie* says: "Jasper gave his soldiers the strictest warlike discipline so that they were neither to curse nor swear nor to make havoc and spoil."

We may compare this with the way in which Lear defends the character of his knights:

> My train are men of choice and rarest parts,
> That all particulars of duty know,
> And in the utmost exact regard support
> The worships of their name[1].

Even more striking is the fact that Goneril states, as a reason for objecting to Lear's knights, that they give Lear the power to raise a conspiracy and to hold Goneril and Albany at his mercy; Albany protests against this view and tells Goneril she may "fear too far," upon which she retorts that it is better than trusting too far.

It is the exact argument that Catherine de Médici used in relation to Coligny; Charles IX wished to spare him and Catherine persuaded the reluctant king that Coligny's nobles were a danger to the royal family as he might put himself at the head of these Huguenots and seize control of the city. The plea was absurd but it served its purpose.

It is notable that the curses Lear utters upon Goneril seem exactly applicable to Catherine de Médici. He first curses her with sterility:

> from her derogate body never spring
> A babe to honour her!

[1] I. iv.

he then adds:

> If she must teem,
> Create her child of spleen; that it may live
> And be a thwart disnatured torment to her!

This almost exactly reproduces the destiny of Catherine who was sterile for a long time after her marriage and whose children grew up to conflicts with her, to bitter jealousies among themselves and to be one of the most evil broods who ever cursed France.

A Huguenot tract published at Basle in 1573 reads:

> Je vous laisse à penser de quel naturel peuvent estre ses enfans, qui sont nourris de son laict...pour le comble de tout malheur, elle les a faits instruments de leur ruine, de l'estat et de la couronne.

The tract goes on to curse them quite in Lear's manner as "les tyrans les plus horribles et les traitres le plus felons qui ont esté, sont et serons à jamais," and wishes that they and all their posterity may be banished from human society.

One curious detail may be noticed here. The tract to which I have already referred (Basle 1573) says that the Huguenots caused:

> faire un tableau...où le cardinal de Lorraine, la Royne sa niece, la Royne mere et la duchesse de Guise estoyent peints au vif nuds, ayans les bras au cols, et les jambes entreslaces l'un avec l'autre.

They found means of sending it into the chamber of the Cardinal when he was holding a Council; the picture was unpacked and all those present saw and understood the deadly insult. This insult was supposed to have had a most untoward result upon the fortunes of the Huguenots.

Here we notice that in Protestant opinion the Cardinal of Lorraine, Catherine de Médici and Mary Queen of Scots were all knitted together in one nude tangle of licentiousness, adultery and incest, making them absolute monstrosities. We may compare this with the terrible passage in which Lear says of his daughters[1]:

> The fitchew, nor the soilèd horse goes to 't
> With a more riotous appetite.
> Down from the waist they are Centaurs,
> Though women all above:
> But to the girdle do the gods inherit,
> Beneath is all the fiends';
> There's hell, there's darkness, there's the sulphurous pit,
> Burning, scalding, stench, consumption.

Nothing like this, of course, is found in the *Chronicle* sources of Lear; but it does represent precisely the way in which the Protestants regarded Mary, Queen of Scots, and Catherine de Médici.

Coligny was also insulted by the cutting down of his retinue. As head of a house which had certain royal privileges he was allowed a hundred nobles as his attendants. In 1569 he was insulted by being ordered to cut down his retinue from a hundred to fifty lances. Lear was, of course, allowed precisely a hundred knights and Goneril proposed to cut them down to fifty.

When Coligny was left alone, robbed by death or treachery of all his supporters, Joan of Navarre stood by him in his darkest hour and she alone sustained him.

We may observe that at the battle of Moncontour in 1569 an incident happened which is a close parallel to King Lear. Coligny was severely wounded by a pistol discharged in his face which shattered his jaw; he maintained himself unflinchingly in his saddle, despite the agony of his wound, but the Huguenots were defeated and a great massacre took place.

[1] IV. vi.

D'Aubigné sums up the matter[1]:

The Admiral saw falling to his share, blame for accidents, silence as to merits. He saw too the remnant of an army which, even before the last disaster, had been in unutterable despair—towns feeble, garrisons fearful, enemies powerful and without pity—least of all for him.

This aged sire, unable to articulate from his wound, shaken with fever, suffering from the thought of afflictions, which thoughts agonised him worse than his wound, was carried from the field in a litter in danger of death. He found himself abandoned by all the great except a woman, Joan of Navarre who, having of woman only the name, had advanced to Niort to stretch out her hand to the afflicted and to deal with affairs.

A modern historian[2] has described the same situation:

The admiral, grievously wounded and unable to articulate was conveyed to Niort in a litter....Confined to his couch and unable to justify himself by word, or by action, Coligny's agitation of mind threatened alarming results. Relief, however, was already on the road to the camp. The tidings of the defeat of Moncontour were no sooner received by her than Jeanne d'Albret quitted La Rochelle and, attended only by her usual suite of gentlemen, she traversed the country, beset by perils innumerable and safely arrived at Niort. Coligny received the queen as an angel sent from heaven to his rescue; and tears bedewed the cheeks of the stern warrior as he clasped the royal hand stretched so compassionately towards him. The admiral was deserted by his officers and nobles who showed no pity for his deplorable condition....

Jeanne's indignation was greatly excited at the isolation of the admiral and she publicly expressed her opinion of the selfish ingratitude of his officers...her presence and support cheered the admiral and exercised the most beneficial effect upon his health[3].

Now here we surely have the closest parallels to Lear. Coligny is carried in a litter, stricken almost to death, unable to articulate, deserted by his followers, accused of impru-

[1] *Histoire Universelle*, III. [2] M. W. Freer.
[3] See also Davila, *Les Guerres Civiles*.

dence, fevered and almost wandering in mind and in an agony of mental suffering that threatens his life. Joan of Navarre appears, venturing in the midst of many perils, and is received almost as an angel of heaven by Coligny.

So is Lear carried in a litter, so is he deserted by almost all, so is he unable to articulate, fevered in mind and in an agony of mental suffering that threatens his very life; so does Cordelia go to his rescue, venturing in the midst of many perils and so did she appear to him as if from another world:

> You are a spirit, I know: when did you die?

Coligny kissed the hand of Joan and Lear wished to kneel to Cordelia; Coligny wept at the meeting and so did Lear, for he said:

> mine own tears
> Do scald like molten lead.

Joan of Navarre expresses her anger at seeing Coligny so deserted, and Cordelia expressed her anger at seeing Lear so deserted. Does it make this scene any the less nobly beautiful to know that it really happened and that the fate of a great nation turned on it?

The doctor whom Joan of Navarre brought to Coligny was Ambrose Paré, the most famous surgeon of his time; he made many improvements in medicine; he also made many improvements in the treatment of the insane, in place of the old brutality substituting a gentler treatment in which music played an important part. So the doctor whom Cordelia brings to Lear tries music for his cure and is a master of gentleness and sympathy. Such traits would be in themselves sufficient to identify the humanest and greatest physician of France.

The Huguenots repeatedly termed Coligny the father of

his country torn in pieces by his ungrateful children. Thus, in the *Memoirs* one of the epitaphs signed "N. M." includes the lines:

Proh scelus, hoc prohibes, patriæ patria impia patrem
Sævis dilanians unguibus ipsa tuis.

The impious country with her fierce nails rends her father.

We may compare this with what Gloucester says to Goneril when he takes Lear away[1]:

Because I would not see thy cruel nails
Pluck out his poor old eyes; nor thy fierce sister
In his anointed flesh stick boarish fangs.

The epitaph goes on to speak of the sufferings of Coligny's body from water and from fire, neither drowned nor consumed and finally hung up on the gallows:

Optarunt sepelire nefas hoc flumina tantum,
Optavit tantum flamma piare nefas.
Lacerum, mersum arbustumque cadaver,
Tandem appendit barbara turba cruci.

So also is Lear's body exposed to water and fire, and finally bound, as he puts it, on a "wheel of his own pain."

You cataracts and hurricanoes, spout
     *   *   *   *   *   *
You sulphurous and thought-executing fires...
Singe my white head[2]!

Another epitaph, signed "A. F. P.," runs:

Et terra et ponto passus discrimina mille,
Aere jactatur Gasparus in vacuo,
Scilicet ut tellus ingens et pontus et aer
Tantam conclament undique sævitiem.
     *   *   *   *   *   *
Terra negata tibi nequaquam, Gaspare, terræ
Ipse negaris; eras cœlesti ab origine totus;
Te totum voluit cœlum, nil terra recepit.

[1] III. vii.   [2] III. ii.

Coligny has suffered much on earth and sea and tossed in the empty air; the great earth itself, ocean and air alike cry out on the fierceness shown to him; it is, in vain, however, that the shelter of the earth was denied; heaven itself claims him. So Lear suffers from all the elements of air, earth, water and fire and counts them less cruel than his children:

> Nor rain, wind, thunder, fire are my daughters.
> I tax not you, you elements, with unkindness,

and appeals to heaven as being on his side:

> O heavens,
> If you do love old men,
> if yourselves are old,
> Make it your cause[1].

Another elegy, signed "L. D. N.," identifies Coligny with his country:

> Terra dolens tremuit, diris ululata querelis,
> Heu patria, et patriæ concidit ipse Pater.

The earth shudders with wild lamentations, for the fatherland itself falls with its father. We may compare Lear's

> And thou, all shaking thunder
> Smite flat the thick rotundity o' the world.

Another elegy (L. B. D.) laments the dismembered corpse and the refusal of earth to a hero who yet is worthy of heaven:

> Cœli sunt digni munere, non tumuli.

So we have Lear's pathetic:

> Upon such sacrifices, my Cordelia,
> The gods themselves throw incense[2].

---

[1] II. iv. Compare also D'Aubigné, *Les Tragiques*, "Le corps tout feu dedans, tout glacé par dehors, Demande la bière et bien tost est faict corps." He is speaking of France.
[2] v. iii.

Another elegy identifies Coligny as France itself; now he is deprived of head, hands and feet, what can prevent the ruin and fall of France? S. M. M.

> Quid mirum si trunca pedesque manusque caputque,
> Patre suo extincto Gallia prona ruit?
> Quid mirum si tota ruit viduata cerebro?
>   *   *   *   *   *   *
> Quid mirum si stare nequit, si labitur expes?
>   *   *   *   *   *   *
> Gaspar, quod si firme tuo tu stante manebas?
> Gaspare, quid mirum si pereunte peris?

There follows an invocation to France:

> Crede mihi, veri si me non fallit imago,
> Hic certa exitii pendet imago tui.

France, widowed of her own brain, will fall to destruction. How can France stand when she has no feet? France herself is hung aloft in the image of Coligny.

This passage is particularly interesting as showing how Shakespeare may have meant his Lear, in some degree at least, as a symbol of France herself, of Lear's loss of his mind as France, "widowed of her brain," while the whole idea of France slipping and falling to destruction suggests a possible meaning for Gloucester and the precipice scene a meaning which, as we shall see, is confirmed also by passages in P. Mathieu.

The lines about Coligny's loss of his head suggest a really terrible meaning for the fool's comparison of Lear to "the hedge-sparrow that fed the cuckoo so long that it had its head bit off by its young," and of Lear's own comparison:

> Is it not as this mouth should tear this hand
> For lifting food to 't[1]?

[1] III. iv. Compare also Agrippa d'Aubigné, *Les Tragiques*: "Ton chef mange tes bras, c'est une faim trop grande...c'est indice de mort." (He speaks of France.)

A. C. M. is another writer who completely identifies Coligny with France. While he lived he was, as it were, the genius of France and, now that he is dead, France is the corpse of France:

> Cujus sit petis hæc imago? cujus
> Casu Gallia, Galliæ est imago.
>
> *   *   *   *   *
>
> Hic est Gasparus ille qui fuit, dum
> Vixit, Gallia Galliæ, perempto
> Illo, Gallia Galliæ est cadaver.

Lear's death is the passing of a whole era in French history, of the extinction of a whole generation of the heroic French Protestants; but in the person of Edgar or Henry of Navarre the new era steps in and takes their place.

A. M. S. declares that Coligny had lived only for France and would gladly have died for her. Fiercely like a beast she has destroyed him, but while he stood she stood also and when he falls she too falls; she owed her happiness to him and will owe her misery to herself. Here again we have a close parallel with Lear; Lear has been devoted to his daughters and has given all to them. They destroy him with brutish ferocity and they also destroy themselves. The continued idea of the fall and of the whole of France falling suggests again the precipice motive:

> Vita ego vivus eram tibi Gallia; mortuus ah mors
> Sum tibi, quem volui vivere morte mea.
>
> *   *   *   *   *   *
>
> Tu me stabas stante, cadente cadis.
> Extinxti me téque simul, fera Gallia.

So also in *King Lear* are victim and persecutor extinguished together.

I could quote many more of these elegies but the central idea is nearly always the same. Coligny is the father of his country betrayed and murdered by his ungrateful children;

his naked body is exposed, deserted and defenceless, to all the outrages of the elements which are still less cruel than his children; Coligny is the genius of France, he is France itself, in his person all France is naked, all France is outraged, all France falls headlong to destruction, all France is slain. None the less she will revive and live again.

Is it possible to avoid seeing the parallel with King Lear; the father who has given all for his children, who would serve them to his last breath, who is exposed naked to all the assaults of the elements, who loses his brain (a really appalling metaphor), and perishes of his own excess of trust and of the black treachery of those he trusted? N. C. M. speaks bitterly of the fraud and guile by which he was destroyed:

> Victus inaudita fraude doloque jacet.

A. D. D. cries that he lived for France and perished in his endeavours to serve her; by her fury against him she has become the tomb both of him and of herself:

> Il vivoit à la France, en la France vivant,
> Il est mort à la France, à la France servant.
> *   *   *   *   *   *
> La France est le tombeau de lui et d'elle-mesme.

The same poem goes on to declare that the man who had risked his head a hundred times for France is now without head:

> Celuy qui pour la France a sa teste cent fois
> Exposé à la mort, sans teste tu vois.
> *   *   *   *   *   *
> Va, France, ingrate! va.

It is, incessantly, repeatedly, over and over again, the great situation of King Lear: the father who has given all for his children and trusted them wholly, the hideous treachery, the hideous ingratitude, the naked body exposed to the outrages of all the elements and France destroying herself and perishing with him.

The elegies on the Queen of Navarre are no less instructive:

> Dum mens continuo cœlestia spirat, anhelum
> Deficiens corpus cessit, humique jacet.

We may compare it with the immortal lines:

> She's dead as earth.
> Why should a dog, a horse, a rat have life
> And thou no breath at all?

Another elegy by G. O. F. reads:

> Vixi: quemque mihi cursum mea fata dedere,
> Per sævam belli rabiem, perque invida mundi
> Crimina, jam per te felix et tuta peregi.

So had Cordelia passed through the fierce rage of war and the "invida crimina" of the world, so had she passed happily and safely beyond; even before she dies Lear takes her for a "soul in bliss" and is sure that the gods throw incense on her sacrifice.

So also with S. P.:

> Nam sibi non fuerat, patriæ sed nata juvandæ.
> *   *   *   *   *   *
> Quæ patriæ vixit, nec sibi nata fuit.

She did not live for herself but was born for her fatherland, she lived for her fatherland and was not born for herself.

Surely it is the epitaph of Cordelia?

I have before pointed out that, after Coligny's death, he was judged and condemned and hanged in effigy; his castle was to be burnt and all his furniture.

It is this piece of absurdity, the judgment of the effigy and the punishment of the furniture, which, I believe, is satirised by Shakespeare in the trial of the joint-stools[1].

---

[1] III. vi.

Lear, representing France in its mood of insanity, appoints
Edgar the madman and the Fool as judges; they sing insane
songs and judge the furniture guilty. Could there be a more
appalling satire on the historic scene?

In *King Lear* we have further the fact that Albany is not
in sympathy with Goneril; he reverences Lear and protests
against Goneril's cruelty; he gives way to her out of love
and because of his own weakness, but he feels pity for his
victim and ultimately relents and repudiates Goneril.
Cornwall, on the other hand, is wholly in sympathy with
Regan and eager to persecute Lear. This, again, is true to
the historical situation. Charles IX loved and reverenced
Coligny; he was too weak to combat his mother and his
brother, but he protested at the time and afterwards re-
pented his share of the tragedy. On the other hand his
younger brother—the Duke of Anjou—was a willing ac-
complice in all. Cornwall, we may remember, was stabbed
by one of his own servants who revolted against him, and
this was precisely the fate that did befall Anjou when he
was Henry III. He died by the dagger of Jacques Clement.

Throughout the drama there is continual talk of dissen-
sions between Albany and Cornwall:

> There is division,
> Although as yet the face of it be cover'd
> With mutual cunning, 'twixt Albany and Cornwall[1].

This exactly expresses the state of affairs between the
Valois princes, for Charles IX continually suspected his
brother—Anjou—of plotting against him.

P. Mathieu in his *Deplorable Death of Henry IV* [2] also sheds
much light on *King Lear*. I cannot help believing that he
had read the drama and understood it.

---

[1] III. i.   [2] 1610. Translated 1612.

He speaks of his master—Henry:

> As his breeding had inured his body to travail...fortune had made his mind invincible to accidents...in the end she was forced to confess that his courage did surpass the violence of her attempts[1].

Mathieu says of Henry's privations in the civil war "that which will hardly be credited in another age, he had some difficulty...to repel hunger which doth never force kings." And again, "He felt a great delight to have reduced life to that point, as no cross of fortune might alter her."

Mathieu speaks of the contempt universally felt for Henry III and the rivalry of his two possible heirs—Navarre and Guise:

> They did no more look of him (Henry III) but as the sunset of his realm; all mens eyes were turned upon two princes, both great in courage and in reputation. The one had a Crown already and the law of the kingdom called him to a second; the other had great parties to get it and to keep it being gotten.
>
> The heart of the one was inclined to love the other, they were seen in one chamber in the Louvre, they went a-hunting, made matches at tennis, played at Dice, visited the ladies together. The King of Navarre carried the Duke of Guise behind him on horseback through the streets of Paris: he loved him as his kinsman...this love degenerating into hatred was the cause of great ruins as we shall see.

Now here we surely have a close parallel to the relations of Edmund and Edgar who are brothers, but whose fraternal love turns to the bitterest opposition. We have the misfortunes of Henry of Navarre, his hard toils of mind and body, his poverty and hunger, but his unfailing courage. We have the contest between the two princes, both claiming the crown of France, one having legal right on his side, the other possessing a strong party.

"These two," says Mathieu of Navarre and Guise, "were the greatest personages that France ever bear and two of the greatest captains in the world....The King (i.e. Henry III)

---

[1] Grimstone's Translation 1612.

suffered the one to force him to make war upon the other....
Henry, notwithstanding, came to the rescue of the king."

Now here again we have parallels to *King Lear*; Edmund
is certainly a great captain and leader just as Guise was a
great captain and leader. Gloucester suffered one of his
sons—Edmund—to turn him against the other—Edgar—
just as the king suffered Guise to turn him against Navarre.
Navarre, notwithstanding this, came to the rescue of the
king in his affliction in spite of the fact that the king had
made war upon him and when Henry III in his exile from
his capital had no one to turn to but Navarre; so does Edgar
come to the rescue of Gloucester when Gloucester is outcast,
deserted and in affliction.

P. Mathieu explains that Navarre was confined in the
court where his life was in danger, but he escaped and fled.
So also was Edgar's life in danger from his father's fomented
wrath against him, so does he escape and flee.

The reader will remember Edmund's method of effecting
the alienation; by a feint he gets Edgar to draw his sword
upon him, then pretends Edgar was attacking his father.
So did Guise attack the Protestant party—Henry among
them—and then pretend that they were making war on
the king. Mathieu explains that Guise's real object was the
death of Henry III and his own seizure of the crown; so of
course Edmund's object was to dispossess his father and to
seize the power of Gloucester which he did.

We may observe, incidentally, Gloucester's curious belief
in astrology which is exactly like that of Henry III.

Mathieu just like D'Aubigné and the authors of the
Memoirs compares the civil wars to a tempest sweeping
France. Navarre was exposed to these tempests, bore the
brunt of them, and, of course, suffered severely[1].

---

[1] The "storm" recurs three times in *King Lear* and so did the
civil wars in France.

In his *Panegyric of Henry IV*, Mathieu further writes concerning the civil war:

> This war taught him great lessons of patience, constancy and frugality....His presence did revive their daunted spirits... who would no more serve a cause miserably dejected, condemned by the king's edicts and pursued with public hatred.... His virtue did not exempt him from the outrages of necessity.

Here again we have a situation resembling that of the outcast Edgar who never loses his courage but sustains his companions in misfortune in all "the outrages of necessity." It is more than probable that Edgar's miserable condition is meant to typify the miserable sufferings of that younger generation of France. D'Aubigné repeatedly terms France frenzied and mad[1] with her sufferings, and so Edgar appears as a Tom o' Bedlam. Edgar says of himself that he eats "the swimming frog, the toad, the wallnewt—swallows the old rat and the ditch-dog[2]." He even says that he eats "sallets of dung." This was literally and truly the diet of the wretched people at the siege of Sancerre, and on many other occasions; D'Aubigné gives a list including Shakespeare's items and many more fearful still; he specially refers to "the excrements of men and animals."

As for the faults of which Edgar accuses himself they were exactly the faults of Navarre: they are the faults of lust and gaming:

> one that slept in the contriving of lust and waked to do it: wine loved I deeply, dice dearly; and in woman out-paramoured the Turk.
> ...Let not the creaking of shoes nor the rustling of silks betray thy poor heart to woman; keep thy foot out of brothels, thy hand out of plackets.

---

[1] *Les Tragiques.*   [2] III. iv.

Mathieu says of the murder of Henry III of France:

That fearful blow did strike France to the heart and reduced it to that estate, as if it had not been speedily supported by that great Prince, it had fallen in pieces. He received her and cherished her as if he had been born for France and not France for him.

Now here we surely have the closest possible parallel to the central episode in the Gloucester story. Gloucester like France has been sorely wounded; he wishes to cast himself over a precipice just as France was in danger of falling in pieces. It is just then that Edgar receives and cherishes him as if he were the parent and Gloucester the child, precisely as Navarre receives and cherishes France.

Mathieu continues:

What other spirit than his would have been capable to temper the passions of mens minds? What Ulysses could have contained so many contrary winds in one bottle? And yet in the midst of all this his heart is firm and his soul quiet.

Here again we have the metaphor of the terrible tempests and Navarre's constancy in the midst of them.

Mathieu continues:

France which during her sleepy and insensible stupidity, had suffered her members to be cut off by pieces, began to open her eyes which she had kept shut, for that she would not know her own miseries nor feel her infirmities and now that she feels her own wounds she desires to be cured.

He speaks of Henry's success in succouring France:

This feeling was the infallible crisis of the country's health; hope revived good men and confusion amazed the wicked.

This body had yet some sound, vigorous and perfect parts and it had good blood to restore it.

Here again we surely have a mythology as closely as possible resembling Shakespeare's Gloucester story. France suffers hideous mutilation, the country is blind; but Henry comes with his succour and brings renewed hope.

This surely is the story of Gloucester?

Nor is this all! Everyone remembers the extraordinary apparition of the devil which Edgar pretends that he has seen and who has just departed. As Edgar represents it, it was the devil who had tempted Gloucester to cast himself over the precipice, but who had let go of his prey or at least had departed from him leaving him still sound.

This again appears to me to be plainly an allusion to the story of Henry III.

He was quite commonly accused by the Guisards his enemies of having given himself into the power of the devil and was in fact identified by them with the devil prophesied in the Apocrypha. There is an extraordinary pamphlet entitled: "Les Propheties Merveilleuses advenues à l'endroit de Henry de Valois...jadis Roy de France," and published in 1589.

This pamphlet declares that Henry III was exactly the devil prophesied in the ninth chapter of the second book of Maccabees.

He was therefore so wholly evil that

il meritoit aussi estre privé de sa couronne et sceptre, et qu'il fust chassé comme indigne de regner, et vivre en quelque lieu retiré, ou bien d'estre envoyé en exil et d'estre puni rigoureusement.

Now Gloucester actually is "chased out" as unworthy of reigning, he has to live in a retired place, he is sent in exile; but Shakespeare like most Englishmen took the part of the unhappy king and represents him as tempted by the devil and almost destroyed but nevertheless escaping.

Also without doubt, just as in P. Mathieu's interpretation, France is symbolised in his person. Henry of Navarre succours him and succours France in him.

Another significant detail is that, when Edgar comes to
the rescue of Gloucester, he pretends to be a peasant and
speaks in a strongly marked southern dialect. Now why?
I have seen no rational explanation of this.

If Edgar, however, is really Navarre the explanation is
perfectly simple; Navarre was brought up in his early life
as a peasant among peasants, he was so markedly a peasant
in his hardiness and endurance that he was called by his
enemies *le roi montagnard* and he spoke in a strong southern
dialect, the dialect of his own Béarn.

The peasant with the strong southern dialect who is also
a great noble and prince is a clear identification of Henry
of Navarre.

Mathieu says again of Henry:

> He hath brought France to a more happy estate than she
> herself durst hope for, whereas having scarce either pulse or
> spirit, after the death of the late king, she cast herself in his
> arms.

It is always the same metaphor, always the symbolism
like that of Shakespeare—France reduced to the last extremity and saved by Henry alone[1].

Mathieu observes that France had suffered so much in
the civil wars "that it became a retreat of wild beasts which
durst not go into the forests," and he speaks of the abun-
dance of the wolves. D'Aubigné in *Les Tragiques* says repeatedly that men themselves seemed turned into wolves
and tigers. We have again the same symbolism in *King
Lear* where Goneril and Regan are compared to wolves and
boars and tigers.

---

[1] Compare also D'Aubigné:

c'est toy qui as porté
A tes juges, proscrit, le présent de la vie:
Ils ont par toy, banni, recouvré la patrie,
De toy, leur prisonnier, receu la liberté.

(He speaks of Henry.)

And now what is the final conclusion to be?

I find it to be in the case of *Macbeth* and *King Lear* exactly as in the case of *Hamlet*, that Shakespeare is really writing of his own age and that his work is a kind of symbolic mythology. The reason we have ignored it so long is because, as I have already explained, we assumed there was no essential difference between the psychology of the sixteenth century and the psychology of the nineteenth. The method of symbolic mythology which I find in Shakespeare is simply the method of his age.

The whole of Spenser's *Faerie Queene* is precisely such symbolic mythology; so are most of Lyly's plays; so in all probability is Sidney's *Arcadia*. So are Ben Jonson's *Masques*. So is much of Drayton.

The historians themselves slip into it at every turn. We find it quite unmistakably in Buchanan's *Detection* and *Oration*.

It is the same with the Frenchmen, D'Aubigné, Ronsard and Malherbe, whose poems are full of such symbolic mythology; it invades the histories of D'Aubigné and De Thou; P. Mathieu writes works, ostensibly historical, which are one mass of such symbolism. The *Memoires* so often referred to write historical prose on one page and the same material, turned into mythological poetry, on the next page.

It is only by studying the mentality of Shakespeare's contemporaries that we can understand the mentality of Shakespeare himself.

I cannot but say that I think we much under-estimate his meaning and with the meaning the terror and beauty and splendour of his work.

APPENDICES

APPENDIX A. THE SCOTTISH WITCH-TRIALS

Miss Margaret Murray's book on *The Witch-Cult in Western Europe* has appeared since I wrote the above chapter. It gives, I think, confirmatory evidence of very great value.

Miss Murray believes that the witches were grouped in "covens" usually numbering twelve members and that each coven had an actual living person who was its "devil." She further believes that the "devil" of the North-Berwick witches was Francis, Earl Bothwell and that his real aim was to gain the crown for himself. One of the most pertinent passages runs as follows:

> Every one, including James, respected Bothwell. Even if they did not acknowledge his divinity, they feared the magical powers which, as Chief of the Witches, he was supposed to wield. It is impossible to study the details of this period without realising the extraordinary fear which James had of his cousin; it was fear with an underlying horror, totally different from his feeling towards his other turbulent subjects. When Bothwell, seeking pardon, was introduced into Holyrood Palace by Lady Athol in the early morning of July 24, 1593, he entered the King's chamber...."The king...asked what they meant. Came they to seek his life? let them take it—they would not get his soul." This remark, made in the urgency and excitement of the moment, is highly significant. Had Bothwell been, like many of James's other enemies, merely an assassin, James would not have spoken of his soul. But Bothwell as the Devil of the witches had the right to demand the yielding of the soul, and James was aware of the fact.

A circumstance of this kind, of course, sheds a still more terrible light on the superstitious horror with which Bothwell would be regarded by the king.

APPENDIX B.   ARIEL

PIERRE MATHIEU says of Henry (Panegyre):

He had need of as many eyes as Argos to watch...as many Armes as Briareus to labour....It seemed that his Canons and regiments had wings, having marched above a hundred and fifty leagues in two months. His counsels pass the wisdom of those that counsel him, his designs prevent the foresight of his enemies....

This Prince was an Eagle in warre which soared into the clouds when they thought to take him and fell suddenly upon them which held him to be further off.

...He casts the firebrand of war upon those who had set France on fire....He strikes everywhere as soon as he threatens. He seems to be mounted on Pegasus, to be in all places where his presence is necessary...his authority like a spirit of life disperseth itself throughout all the members of the body....Artillery is an invention so new, so terrible and so different from all the ancient engins, as we may say that at these days we make war not with iron, as in former time, but with fire, not with violent force, but with wisdom....

His forehead glistering like a Comet at the encounter of Fountaine Francoise, forced the Constable of Castile to flee...he clipped the wings of victory to the end that she should not fly out of France.

(This is surely a most illuminating phrase!)

Mathieu says again:

The lightning which should be feared of those which are not touched with it, is ready to fall. Justice shows the lightnings afar off, valour causeth the thunder to be felt....His canons, echoing in the Alps amazeth all Italy....The Ambassadors... were so amazed as they thought that enchantment, taking from them the true substance of that which they sought, had substituted a fancy.

In the poem attached to the Panegyric Mathieu says:

> In Ivry fields he seems a blazing star.
> Who least fear him, on them first he falls.
>
> .   .   .   .
>
> He that commanded Victorie at will.
>
> (Grimstone's Translation 1612.)

Henry's own letters often contain similar phrases, as when he entreats his friends to "fly" to battle "swifter than air."

I propose to deal with this subject later. Here it is only necessary to point out that Ariel seems to embody the essential qualities of Henry's genius as Pierre Mathieu saw them: the air-like swiftness, the flight through the air (like Pegasus), the unexpected appearances (like an eagle), the all-observant watchfulness (eyed like Argus), the foresight and prevention, the fiery force, the meteor-like brilliancy, the unexpectedness and swiftness which are so great that they appear like enchantment.

There is doubtless more in Ariel than this, but I am convinced that it is one meaning of the character.

INDEX